BETSEY.

BETSEY.

A Memoir

· · · · · · · ·

Betsey Johnson
with Mark Vitulano

VIKING

VIKING

An imprint of Penguin Random House LLC
penguinrandomhouse.com

Pages 271–72 constitute an extension to this copyright page.

ISBN 9780525561415 (hardcover)
ISBN 9780525561422 (ebook)

Printed in the United States of America
1   3   5   7   9   10   8   6   4   2

Designed by Cassandra Garruzzo

Contents

HEY!!!
GIRLFRIENDS ɪN'
BOY FRIENDS!
"+ KIDDOS OF ALL AGES!
"THANK YOU"
FOR BUYIN' MY BOOK!
I HOPE YOU
LIKE it!
XOX
BETSEY.

ow, to you it may be just a book. But to me, it's my life. And *that* is scary.

I could have written this memoir years ago. In fact, I tried to, and it didn't work out. I don't think I was ready.

But now I'm at a point in time where I have some perspective and am able to look closely. A point where I finally feel I have the courage to draw back the curtains and see what's behind them; the good, the bad, *and* the hard to look at.

This book is also a way for me to give back; something for the generations of devoted Betsey girls.

Everyone knows me by the cartwheels, the splits, the crazy hair, and the sexy clothes.

But I want people to see there is a real person behind the persona I've spent years creating. And also to know that there is a method to my madness, and who knows, maybe learn some life lessons along the way.

So what do you say? Let's lace up our roller skates and go for a ride!

xoX
Betsey.

BETSEY.

1.) A WHITE PICKET FENCE: THE EARLY YEARS.

To go back to the very beginning, I was born on August 10, 1942, in Wethersfield, Connecticut, a small suburb of Hartford. That date put both my sun and moon in the sign of Leo. Now, I don't take astrology *too* seriously. I don't make daily decisions based on charts or planets or any of that. But there's no denying that from the time I was little, my Leo personality was in full bloom.

From what I've heard, the sun in Leo means you go out into the world and you shine. And that behavior was always instinctual to me. I was full of energy and enthusiasm and had my own special kind of appeal that wasn't at all determined by my looks. I was never the kind

of pretty that would make every head turn when I walked into a room. That's for sure.

Instead, I relied on my bubbly, oddball personality to make my way in the world. I distinctly remember one instance of that from when I was a child. I was home after school. My sister and brother were at opposite ends of the living room, both studiously doing their homework. I walked into the room and out again and back again—the whole time walking on my *hands*, my feet in the air swaying as I tried to keep my balance. I kept this up for more than thirty minutes until my mother finally toppled me over and said, "Betsey Lee! Stop that!" I looked up at her from the floor confused and said, "I can't. It's not perfect yet." That was my peculiar drive in a nutshell.

As bubbly as I may have been, I was also what my mother called a "worrywart," which I thought sounded so ugly. But she was right: I would literally lie in bed at night and fret. It wasn't just the typical monster-under-the-bed situation. I was just an insecure, scared little girl.

I remember I had this irrational fear of dying, which came seemingly from nowhere. My mother would ask me what I was so worried about, and I didn't know how to answer. What made it all the worse was that I didn't even know *how* to talk about it. The fear was very real to me. I couldn't accept that I was actually going to die in the end—whatever and whenever the end might be. I used to tell my mom: I better not die before Christmas, which was my favorite time of year. My mother, in her own way trying to reassure me, would say, "We are *all* going to die . . . someday." I didn't feel any better. Her response just fueled my anxiety.

If I were to play armchair psychiatrist, I would have to say that World War II had something to do with my dread. The war was in full swing when I was born. I do remember hearing war reports on the radio as a child and seeing scary pictures in the newspaper that I didn't quite understand.

The war didn't directly threaten our safe little corner of Connecticut. But I guess the specter of some kind of Nazi bogeyman permeated the collective consciousness in a way that even little children couldn't escape it. My father would tell us stories of his role during the conflict. He was what was known as a "blackout man," responsible for going around the neighborhood and making sure everyone had their blackout shades down after sunset. I found it creepy that my dad—who was sweet, kind, and so full of life—had to make sure everyone in town was sealed into darkness every night.

I could also attribute my anxiety to the moon-in-Leo part of my nature. And by that I mean, when my Leo moon would kick in, oh crumb! It would come along with a pail of water to pour all over my sunny-side up. From very early on I understood that I had a choice: did I want to choose the light or the dark? I wanted the happiness and sunshine. I usually found it easy enough to shake off the dark and get back into the light.

Wethersfield was at that time a very small, tight-knit

community—the type of place that had neighborhood vegetable gardens and where everyone knew everyone else. Women would get together once a week for sewing bees. My mother actually hated sewing but she joined in to be sociable . . . and to learn to sew clothes for her children. It was cheaper for her to make our clothes than to go out to a department store to buy them.

Every year she'd make matching back-to-school dresses for me and my sister. They were always plaid and had little puff sleeves and sashes and bows. She later also sewed all of my dancing costumes, and I started to help. I had no idea that this would become my life's work. Back then it was just a means to an end. I don't remember deriving any great pleasure from cutting and sewing other than the joy of spending time alone with my mom.

I don't know whether my family would have been considered working class or lower middle class. Whatever we were, I just know we weren't fancy. We lived in the classic little house with the white picket fence. Very quaint, very country. Looking back, I see my childhood as very comforting and traditional, a series of endless, sunny summers followed by winters that looked like Christmas cards or a Norman Rockwell painting. We were apple pie to the max.

I had the most wonderful, loving family you can imagine. There was Mom and Dad, and I've already mentioned my brother and sister. By way of a more formal introduction, they are Sally, who was the oldest of the kids, and Bobby, the youngest. Each of us two years apart. When I was really little,

My devilishly dashing daddy, Chick   *My mom, Live Wire Lena*

Me, Bobby, and Sally in our plaid den

we had two kittens, which I named Pete and Re-Pete. In fact, we always had animals around. I remember there was a collie named Lassie (not the most original name), a horse named Scout, and later on another cat who would only eat Cheerios that she would take one at a time from a bowl with her paw.

Sally was the best sister I could ever wish for. She was just so perfect, always doing *good* things. She was the president of her class, she ran the local pool, she volunteered for the Red Cross. Everything she did I wanted to do, too. I guess you could say I idolized her.

Even while my true nature was already pointing me toward a different path, part of me wanted to follow in Sally's footsteps. I sometimes felt that I couldn't keep up with her, and there were definitely periods of animosity and competition. I'd sometimes get so upset with her, which was usually just my own frustration at not being as good as her. I fantasized about sneaking over to her bed while she was sleeping and biting her fingernails off. They were her pride and joy. My high energy level always had me feeling nervous or anxious, so I naturally bit my own nails down to nubs, which left me with aching fingers. I hid my hands a lot.

As for Bobby, he was the typical happy, sweet brother. He was the fastest guy on the basketball team. Basketball wasn't the only sport he was good at. He also had a sharp eye when it came to darts. One time he landed one right into my leg all the way from across the room!

To say that we were an active bunch would be an understatement. Between Cub Scouts, Girl Scouts, dance classes, and baseball practice, we kept Mom and Dad pretty busy carting us around. But they never begrudged us our after-school activities. Quite the opposite—they totally encouraged and supported them.

Mom's name was Lena and Dad's was John, but for some reason everyone called him Chick. They were an idyllic couple. I have never seen two people more in love. I never once remember them having a fight, or if they did, it was never in front of us kids. They had met and married when they were both very young. Mom was petite, wiry, and pretty in a very fifties way, especially when she was all dressed to go out. It didn't happen very often, which made it all the more special to see her that way. Dad, who was a tall, blond, handsome devil, fell in love with her and her vivacious personality.

Dad had gone to Pratt Institute back when it was mostly a technical college. He was trained as an electrical engineer but ended up working at the Taylor & Fenn metal foundry. He made metal patterns for the decorative details you see on things like Winchester rifles and potbellied stoves.

Once when we kids were really young, as a special treat he took us to the factory to show us what he did all day. When I think back on that trip, I can still see those big metal pattern pieces hanging from the ceiling of his workshop, and they remind me of pattern pieces that have hung from the ceilings in my own workrooms over the years.

My mom's job was running the household. And it was a full-time job. But in spite of that, she was also den mother for my brother's Boy Scout troop and my sister's and my Brownie units, and, just for good measure, head of the PTA. Mom was always on the go, just a bundle of nervous energy. I always pictured her as a human vacuum cleaner that was never unplugged. If I inherited one quality from each of my parents, it would have to be my father's *unflinching* work ethic and my mother's *boundless* energy.

When I was about six years old, Dad switched jobs and moved the family ten miles away to Windsor, which was another small Connecticut town. Windsor was less country than Wethersfield, and it was a bit more upscale. No victory gardens there. But we did have tobacco fields. There were no more sewing circles, either, which was just fine with Mom.

The house we moved into was more modern than our previous one—very 1950s. I can still vividly picture the kitchen wallpaper. It was salmon colored with a white lattice design and ivy running through it. And, of course, we had the plaid den complete with Ethan Allen furniture and a black-and-white TV set, which was a big deal. Not everyone had me.

It was very important to Mom and Dad that the whole family have breakfast together every morning, and at six each evening, come hell or high water, no matter how much stuff we kids had going on, we'd sit down to have dinner—that is, except Mom. She buzzed around serving the rest of us. It was light-years away from how things are nowadays.

When we kids were older and didn't need her to watch over us when we got home from school anymore, Mom took a job as a guidance counselor at our school. Can you imagine? If you got into trouble you had to go see my mother. Of course, that was never an issue for me, Sally, and Bobby. For the most part we were *good* kids.

I can remember getting into trouble only a couple of times. Once, when I was about five or six years old, around the time I'd have been learning how to read, I was out in the backyard with my best friend, Vicky. She had perpetually skinned knees and came from a few blocks over where the picket fences weren't quite as white as ours. She also had an older brother who you might say was a bad influence on her.

One day, Vicky dramatically wrote a word on a piece of paper. I couldn't read it, so she told me to sound it out, like we did in school. I looked at the letters and read them aloud one by one. F-U-C-K. She said, "Now put them all together," and I said "fuck." She laughed, and I didn't know why, so I said it again. I had never heard the word before and certainly didn't know what it meant. The word felt so strange in my mouth when I repeated it. Pretty soon Vicky and I were skipping around the yard saying and singing the word over and over. Fuck, fuck, fuck, fuck, fuck, fuck, fuck! We must have been quite a sight, two little girls in patent leather shoes, bobby socks, crinolines, and pigtails, cussing like a couple of sailors.

Unfortunately for me, my father had witnessed the whole

scene from inside the house. He came running out, yelling for Vicky to go home. He dragged me inside and promptly washed my mouth out with soap. If you have never had your mouth washed out with soap, believe me, it is *not* pleasant. But I understood.

I never got an explanation from Dad as to what that word meant and why I should never say it. I was just told that it was bad. Which of course only made me want to say it all the more, but for the rest of my childhood I didn't.

Another incident with Vicky happened about a year later. This time we were in Woolworth's, and she dared me to steal something. It didn't matter what it was, she told me. It was just about stealing or, more accurately, getting away with it. We walked around the store for a while trying to look inconspicuous. My heart was racing while I looked for something to swipe, eventually ending up in the candy section. I surveyed the huge selection of goodies—candy cigarettes, candy necklaces, bubble gum, Charleston Chews, and chocolate bars—before I finally decided on a pack of cherry-flavored Life Savers. I figured they were small and easy to hide, and besides, they were my favorites. I looked around one more time to check that no one was watching and when I was sure I was safe I slipped them quickly into the waistband of my skirt. We nervously made our way toward the front of the store and just as we were about to step outside, I felt a hand on my shoulder and heard a gruff voice saying, "Come with me, miss." I froze and my blood ran cold. My first thought was *I am going to jail.* My second was *My parents are going to kill me for this.*

They let Vicky go home because she hadn't done anything wrong, even though I burst into tears and said that she had made me do it. They hauled me to an office upstairs, called my parents, and told them to come down to the store. The worst part of the whole incident was the shame I felt waiting for them in that scary locked office.

When my parents arrived, they told me that they were disappointed in me, which was more of a disgrace than having my mouth washed out with soap. Their approval meant everything to me.

As punishment, I had to work at the store after school for a week with no pay. Which is strange. It seems like a kid with sticky fingers would be the *last* person you would want working for you. But I'm sure they could tell I wasn't exactly a budding career criminal.

As far as school went, I hated it. I didn't have the temperament to sit through a boring math or science class. Truth is, I just wasn't any good at it. I wasn't book smart at all. That's not to say I didn't do well. My parents were very strict when it came to grades. We were absolutely not allowed to bring home anything less than B's, which meant I had to work harder on some subjects than my classmates. My only real interests in school were all extracurricular: boys, dancing, and, by the time I got to high school, being a cheerleader.

Please note, I listed boys first. That's because I and my girl-friends were absolutely stark raving boy crazy. Foul language and shoplifting aside, we were *good* girls, especially me. No tits, no ass, no makeup, no nuthin'! Like all girls our age we talked a *lot* about sex because it was an exciting but also taboo subject. It was a very scary thing to think about, because we knew so little.

That would change around the age of fourteen, thanks to my new best friend, Sandy Barker. She was the most gorgeous girl on our tiny planet, the real hot chick in town. Unlike the rest of us she had a body and was not afraid to show it. She was *not* a good girl. Also, unlike the rest of us she went out with the bad boys. Bad boys! I mean, how bad could they have been in a small rural town in Connecticut in the mid-1950s?

In spite of her fast reputation, Sandy hung out with us straight arrows, so of course we loved her for that. She'd tell us naughty things now and then, stuff she did with the boys. We believed everything that came out of her mouth, blushing the whole time, of course. We were so green that up till that point in our lives, we literally thought you could get pregnant by sit-ting on a toilet seat and get rid of a pregnancy by taking a pill—until Sandy set us straight.

Thank God for Sandy. Before I met her, everything I knew, or thought I knew about sex, had to be left to a fourteen-year-old girl's imagination. I had to speculate about everything be-cause this was an era when you simply *couldn't* ask your parents. It just wasn't done.

Yup, we were boy crazy all right, but boys—real flesh and blood boys—were a complete mystery to me. They were like fictional characters you would read about in books. There was never any mention of the "P" word or any anatomical talk. The only points of reference we had came from playing with our Ken dolls as kids. That's not to say we didn't chase after boys, we did. We just didn't *understand* them.

When I did start dating, it was all very squeaky clean. I always went for the jocks, which made sense because by that time I was a cheerleader. They were part of my crowd. I remember spending an obscene amount of time preparing for dates. I would iron and starch my petticoats to within an inch of their lives to get them just perfect to wear under the latest ruffly dress Mom still occasionally made for me. When my date arrived, he would come into the house and always had to shake my father's hand and tell him where we were going and what time he would bring me home. I never understood the need for all the questions. Dates were always the same. It was either a movie at the one theater in town or a soda at the one diner. It was all very innocent but it was also exciting to be sticking my big toe into this strange new world.

When I got a bit older, the boys would have cars, and we could get more adventurous. There were lots of little "parking" streets in our neighborhood, dead ends that didn't get much traffic. My parents happened to be out driving one evening when they pulled down one of these streets to turn around and saw me and my on-and-off boyfriend in the front seat of his car making out. They didn't stop, and I had no idea they had driven by, but when I got home, as soon as I came through the door, my mother smacked me and told me what she had seen. I was in shock.

She had never laid a hand on me before or after. Any sort of physical contact, good or bad, was so far out of character for my mother, and my father, for that matter, that it really had an impact on me. I realized just how much she cared about me to do something like that. A little slap on the face showed me that she really cared. She needn't have worried. I had no interest in going any further than, what is it, first base? I mean, I never did anything more than make out with my boyfriends. That said, I secretly vowed to be more discreet in the future.

Enter Ann K. Pimm

While boys did occupy a lot of my time and headspace, the real driving force of my childhood was dance. Almost as soon as I could walk I danced. I danced everywhere: in my bedroom, the living room, the kitchen, in the street on my way to school, everywhere.

I even put on my own recitals in the backyard. My dad would lay down a couple of big sheets of plywood for me to use as my little stage and all of the kids from the neighborhood would come. Admission was a penny, which I collected in a paper bag at the backyard gate.

As I said earlier, I was an anxious kid, but dance changed

"A penny a kiss a penny a hug"—Ann Pimm dance recital

that for me. When I danced I was free from worry. As long as I kept moving, nothing could touch me, which was a dizzying way to go through childhood. Turning reality into a blur! Truth be told, I still like to blur reality.

When I was just four years old, my mother signed me up for dance classes at the only place for them in town: the Ann K. Pimm School of Dance. It may have been a small-town dance school, but Ann was anything but small town. Before moving to Wethersfield she had been a professional dancer. She was the real deal and had appeared on Broadway in *Pal Joey* and *One Touch of Venus*.

Ann was beautiful, glamorous, *and* an amazing dancer. She had dark hair and dark eyes and couldn't have been more than five foot two. A real little spitfire. To me she was like Ava Gardner, Cyd Charisse, and Mitzi Gaynor all rolled into one, with maybe a little bit of Gina Lollobrigida thrown in. Even at such a young age I knew that she was different from all of the other women in Wethersfield, a pretty big fish in a tiny, tiny pond. I figured all the women in town must be jealous of Ann because all the men in town had to be in love with her. I fell totally under her spell.

Every day at school I couldn't wait for that last bell to ring so I could hightail it to Ann's class and start dancing and have all the day's cares and worries just roll right off me as I spun around. Ann taught ballet, tap, and jazz and encouraged gymnastics. I was a natural acrobat and learned to do somersaults, back flips, and, yes . . . cartwheels. Dance class was held most afternoons at the Knights of Columbus hall in the center of Old

Wethersfield. The main meeting hall was a huge space that you could really feel lost in. Each day before class all of us students would line up chairs along the walls so the mothers could sit and watch us as we practiced. When we had the place set up, Ann would make her entrance in the same uniform every single day: a black leotard with a white stiffly starched short, short skirt. I admired that skirt so much and wanted to wear one just like it, but all us girls only got to wear the leotard.

While Ann was a real inspiration as a dancer, she was also very creative when it came to the costumes for our recitals. She turned us into dancing strawberries, butterscotch candies, Neapolitan ice creams. That last costume was my favorite. It featured a brown tulle skirt, a leotard top, and a hat made from a square brown box painted pink, off white, and brown tied under the chin with a pink ribbon. I still have that costume to this day.

Ann's inspiration wasn't limited to the confines of the old Knights of Columbus hall. A couple of times a year she would take a few of her special students on field trips to places I had only heard about or dreamt of. I will always love Ann for showing me New York City for the first time. Even though we lived only two hours away, it might just as well have been a thousand miles. My parents never took us there. My father hated New York with a passion. I never knew why, but he never had one good thing to say about the city.

Our first trip was to Radio City Music Hall to see the Rockettes' Christmas spectacular. As I stood outside the theater my

eyes just bulged out of my head. It was so big and so glamorous. I had never seen a building like it. All of the big buildings
in Wethersfield were kind of scary looking. I especially loved
that grand stairway in the lobby. Ann let us girls walk up and
down and up and down those fairy-tale steps, and we felt just
like movie stars. When it was time to get off the staircase and
into the theater itself, my amazement kicked into high gear.
The Art Deco–style stage shone just like a big, faceted gold
Christmas ornament.

We found our seats just as the lights were going down, and
a minute later the orchestra launched into an overture of a
medley of my favorite Christmas songs. And then the Rockettes themselves came onstage dressed up like toy soldiers with
rosy painted-on cheeks and high hats. But there was more.
They then transformed into elves and by the end were all done
up like reindeer pulling Santa's sleigh. When I saw them form
their famous kick line from my seat, which was way off to the
side of the stage, it looked as if their legs stretched for miles. I
knew right then and there what I wanted to do with my life—
get to New York City and become a Rockette.

I worked hard for that dream. I studied practically every
day with Ann until I was fourteen years old. When my family
and I moved to Windsor, about forty-five minutes away by car,
I needed my mom to drive me to dance practice, which meant I
couldn't go as often.

So what was I going to do if I couldn't dance with Ann five

days a week? Crazy as it sounds, I started running my own dance school. An older girl from Ann's class had opened a studio a few years earlier and then she got married and pregnant. She asked me if I wanted to take over the business. That's how the Betsey Johnson School of Dance was born.

I had learned so much from Ann that I was more than up to the task of teaching solo. Considering all of the girls were quite young, it wasn't very challenging work. I taught only on the weekends, which meant that between school and the studio, I was working seven days a week. The crazy schedule didn't faze me in the least. I was doing what I loved to do, I was also making some money of my own and learning how to handle the financial matters of the school, which Dad helped me with.

High School

Dad moved us one final time to a tiny town called Terryville, about twenty miles west of Wethersfield. I didn't miss a beat when starting at the new school because I was never an outsider. At my previous school I had joined the cheerleading squad, probably in another attempt to keep up with Sally, who had been a cheerleader, too. I had an automatic in with that crowd, joined up, and made friends easily.

Along with cheerleading my other main focus at school was art. From childhood on I could always draw well and loved to

Goody-goody girl. High school yearbook photo, 1959.

do it, but in high school my art rose to a new level. The reason for the boost was my art teacher. Just like Ann Pimm, Rita Card would be a major influence on the direction my life would take. Rita was very creative and recognized that trait in me right off the bat. She really encouraged me to push myself, and when I did, I saw my work gain more depth and get better and better.

And, just like Ann, Rita was an original and stood out in

our rural Connecticut town. She had long straight dark hair, almond-shaped eyes, and perfect pale skin. She could have been a model for a Modigliani painting; very exotic, almost Polynesian looking. Even though she stuck out, she didn't care. She had her own style and owned it.

One of the chief things Rita taught me was how to *look* at an object and really *see* it. Sometimes it was an egg, sometimes a wooden box or a doll. Some days we would spend the entire class just looking at one of these objects, maybe changing the way the light hit it. A lot of the time we never even picked up a pencil. This may sound crazy, but it left its mark on me. It was Rita's direction that got me to focus . . . which was no small feat.

Rita's lessons weren't confined to just the classroom. Again,

From walk-overs onstage . . . to flip-flops on the field

like Ann Pimm, she would take a group of us students on sketching trips around town—much to the dismay of the principal. But Rita didn't care. Being her student was like being in the movie *The Prime of Miss Jean Brodie*. She made us feel like the crème de la crème!

As my senior year in high school was winding down and prom time grew closer, I campaigned for and was named head of the prom committee. I suppose this was another example of my competing with Sally, as two years earlier she had been in charge of decorating her prom. Her theme was "Around the World in 80 Days." Each table was decorated in the style of a different country. The Italian table had a red-and-white-checked tablecloth and Chianti bottles covered in melted wax. The French table had baskets of French bread and a papier-mâché Eiffel Tower. The Irish table was all green and covered in shamrocks cut out of construction paper . . . you get the idea. It was so creative and so well executed. I was in awe of what she had accomplished but never let on to Sally.

Now it was my turn to show what I could do. And what did I choose for my theme? "Flirtation Walk," which is what we used to call a secluded area where your date would take you for a make-out session. It sounds very 1950s to me now—like something right out of the movie *Grease*. As a decorative concept it was vague and abstract to say the least.

The decor consisted mostly of sparkling lights draped around arches that my friends helped me make. I placed the arches all around the gym so all the prom couples could enter together through these magical—or at least twinkling—doorways. The rest of the decorations were balloons, streamers, and bunting all in shades of whites and soft pinks. I had started off wanting to create a fairyland, but it ended up a tacky mess.

On the upside, I was named prom queen. Back then it was less a popularity contest than about being rewarded for decorating the prom. Now homecoming queen, *that* was different. That went to the best-looking girl, and that definitely was *not* me. I'm not saying I wasn't popular. I was very popular, but that was based on my personality, and looking back, I'm glad for that. Looks fade. Personality lasts a whole lot longer.

Back to prom night. I wore a dress that was heavy off-white satin with a floor-length dirndl skirt. The bodice went straight across, and the whole dress was sprinkled with rhinestones and little crystal droplets. Of course, I couldn't leave well enough alone. I added more rhinestones and more droplets. I wore my hair, which I had lightened from my natural dark brown to a bad shade of red, in an updo. And to add insult to injury, my entire face had broken out. I looked awful. Leo and I must have been going through a bad patch, because I don't even remember the name of the boy I went with. All I know is I needed a date, and he asked me. I didn't want to go with him. He had more pimples than I did.

I spent the entire evening checking on the decorations and making adjustments as balloons sagged and bunting dropped to the dance floor. This maintenance was no small feat while wearing that heavy dress, which must have been five feet wide, including petticoats (starched, of course). I couldn't just sit back, relax, and enjoy what was supposed to be a special rite-of-passage night. I had to attack it like I would a job. I don't remember how the night ended except that I made my pimply date stay after and help me put the gym back in order.

So compared to Sally's prom success, mine was an artistic failure. But I didn't beat myself up about it for long. I had already demonstrated my talent and knew what was next after graduation.

The year before, we students had been told that it was time to think about college. I never gave a thought to a school anywhere else but in New York City. And since Dad had gone to Pratt and since Pratt is in New York, it was a no-brainer. Rita Card helped me put together a portfolio of my illustrative artwork, and I applied to Pratt. I got in easily.

New York here I come!

2.) PRATT MADE ME FAT: COLLEGE YEARS

Armed with only black charcoal and a newsprint pad, I was told to draw a happy yellow cube, or a sad pink circle. Or every once in a while just to keep us on our toes, a colorful country scene. Welcome to Pratt Institute!

My parents drove me to the school on one of the last hot days of summer in 1960 to start my new life as a college student. After getting me and my belongings unloaded into my dorm room and saying our tearful goodbyes, they left as quickly as they could for the two-hour drive from Brooklyn back to Terryville. They still didn't like the city. I didn't mind that they didn't stay to get me settled. I was happy to finally be on my own in New York City, just as I had dreamt since Ann Pimm had taken me to see the Rockettes.

But the Rockettes visit seemed like a million years ago. I wasn't a little girl anymore; I was a real-deal college student. So feeling independent and *kind of* like a grown-up I began unpacking my things. I got my clothes sorted out and arranged my dolls on the bed. I know it sounds childish, but against Mom's suggestion that I leave them behind, I brought a few of my favorites with me to remind me of home.

While lost in the task and fantasizing about what my new school life would be like I met my roommate. Back at home I was used to sharing my room with Sally, so having a roommate was no big deal and, luckily, Cheryl and I hit it off right away. She was a pretty blond home-economics major who had been randomly assigned to me. I know that home economics as a major sounds pretty silly today, but in 1960 it was still a legitimate thing.

After a day of orientation my priority was to check out the cheerleading situation. I should have done some research before I got there because I was disappointed to learn that Pratt didn't have a football team. All they had to offer in terms of sports was basketball. After I got to know the school and the other students a little better, I was shocked that they even had that. Pratt was an extremely artsy school even as art schools go, so there was very little competition for cheerleading squad, and I easily managed to get a spot.

A lot of my classmates—mostly the guys, thank you very much—looked down on me for being a cheerleader. They considered it a pretty geeky and even a lame thing to do, something better left to the girls in home ec, like my roommate. They would have been wrong about that as well. Cheryl, as it turned out, wasn't a geek at all. In fact, she was a pretty ballsy chick. She used to sneak out of our room at night while I pretended to be asleep. I didn't let on to anyone, not even her, that I knew she was going AWOL. But it was killing me not knowing what she was doing.

After a few weeks as we got more chummy, she finally confided in me, like roommates do. She told me that practically every night she was going into Manhattan and picking up guys for money. Cheryl was a prostitute. I was shocked but also a

Cheerleading Syracuse—"The Orange Girls," "The Orange Men"

Thunder thighs and pom-poms

little bit intrigued. The only prostitutes I knew about were hard-boiled, bigger-than-life characters I'd seen in movies. Not at all like cute, bright, perky Cheryl. Unfortunately, not long

28

after she shared her secret with me, the school found out about her nightly escapades, and she was thrown out. Such a shame. Not only had our personalities clicked and I sincerely liked Cheryl, but she had kept me fully stocked with pastries created in her cooking classes.

At the same time, I was finding it difficult relating to my art-department classmates. My cheerleading just didn't fit in with their preconceived notion of how an artist should behave. These kids were so pretentious and full of themselves that all of them were convinced they were going to be the next Picasso, and I hated that. I just wanted to do my art and hopefully make a career of it some day.

While I may not have been crazy about some of the students, I did like my teachers, even though they didn't do much to discourage their students' attitudes of superiority. The professors were pretentious, too, but at least they had the degrees and experience to back it up.

In some of my drawing classes, the assignments that we were given were very challenging (the happy yellow cube exercise mentioned above) and seemed to come out of left field. I felt as if the teachers were always trying to confuse us, but what they were really doing was daring us to think in new ways. Trying to get us to see the flip side of things.

In addition to my drawing classes I also had a sculpture class, taught by a teacher who was a real trip. He had long hair, which was almost unheard of back then, and he wore old baggy clothes. He looked like a hippie before hippies even existed. I considered him a great teacher because he was the first person who got me to see things in three dimensions, to notice form and function. He taught me how to use a whole different part of my brain, which I know came into play later when I started designing clothing.

Years later I found myself thinking back on these professors. I connected the dots and realized why some of them were so great. Given that it was 1960 and that we were living in New York City, it made total sense that most of them were beatniks, and that kind of beat attitude naturally spilled over into their teaching.

When I first decided on going to Pratt, I thought that I would be able to take my art classes by day and dance classes at night. I still hadn't given up the dream of becoming a Rockette. That idea went right out the window as soon as school got started. The teachers heaped so much work on us that I barely had enough hours in the day to meet my deadlines. I think that in my heart of hearts I had known that I wasn't going to be able to do both. I realized that if I was going to take dancing seriously I should have gone to a dance school. If Pratt basically put an end to my dancing dreams, the good news was that after looking into the matter, I found out that I was too short to be a Rockette anyway.

As the school year wore on I became disillusioned with Pratt. I was looking for what I had perceived to be a *real* college experience, like the kind I'd seen on TV. I wanted a campus and a football stadium, sororities and the frat parties. And Pratt just didn't have those. My grades were good, I loved my teachers, and I was well liked in *some* crowds, but to be honest, while I had tried my best, I realized that I just didn't like it there. It wasn't only the taunts about my cheerleading and the way-out assignments, it was also the workload. It was simply too much. No one could push me harder than I could push myself; I just didn't like others doing so. I still don't. To make matters worse, I was overeating and ended up putting on a lot of weight. (Thank you, Cheryl, for getting me started with all of those goodies from your cooking classes.) Even with all my physical activity, I kept packing on the pounds. Pratt made me fat!

So right after Christmas break, I made the decision that at the end of the year I would leave the school. The staff wanted me to stay, I was a good student, but when I make up my mind it stays made up. My parents were supportive of my choice to leave and helped me find a new school. I wanted the next one to also be relatively close to home, because I enjoyed taking occasional weekend breaks to visit my family. I looked at Rhode Island School of Design and really liked their art programs, but again, no sports teams. I seriously considered Boston University for a while, but after visiting Syracuse University and seeing their football stadium and the quad, I loved the sheer huge-ness of S.U. So many students to get lost among and the feeling to be free to find my own way. I never felt that at Pratt. The choice was clear. Even though it was over three hours from home, I knew I would still be able to manage family visits.

One of the big changes course-wise at Syracuse was that in addition to my illustration classes, I also was able to study fabric design. Back then fabric design was a pretty weird thing to be into, and there weren't many students in that class. I only ended up there as an extension of my illustration classes. I was looking for skills that would give me some practical application out in the real world and a better chance of landing a job when I graduated.

Not that the fabric design class was perfect. Our assignments were *always* the same: Create repeat patterns. Believe me when I tell you that designing repeats is *so* anal and *so* boring. Repeat, repeat, repeat, over and over again. I could *not* stand it!

Me being me, I could never wrap my head around doing the work in any conventional way. The art department had small printing presses and silkscreens. By this time I had given up my childhood bad habit of biting my nails and now boasted long fingernails, which I started to use on the screens instead of the carving tools provided to us. I would dig my nails right into the silkscreen or linoleum blocks or whatever other material we had and carve my designs, slashing away and creating geometric and abstract prints. But my specialty was, not surprisingly, florals. It was a really messy way to work. I could never quite manage to get all of the ink out from under my nails.

The results of my method were much wilder, abstract, and somehow more modern designs than those that the other students were doing. I was into a more organic, free-form technique than that damned repeat, repeat, repeat. And in a way, I was kind of lazy and wanted to have fun with it. The teachers never questioned my methods. They pretty much left me alone and even encouraged me to do what I wanted as long as I completed the assignments on time and to their satisfaction, which I always did. I had the freedom at Syracuse to be me, whatever *that* was at the time!

My experimentation was supported and eventually rewarded by the department. Ten years after I graduated, I was presented with the George Arents Award, which the university gives once a year to alumni who make good. To commemorate the award, a few of my former professors lobbied to have two of the dorm rooms redecorated with my prints. A plaque outside each of them announced it was "The Betsey Johnson Room."

The prints they chose to decorate the rooms were florals done in extremely vibrant color combinations. I've always been drawn to colors that vibrate when you put them side by side. One of the rooms featured a crazy orange and bright pink pattern, and the other was done in glowing turquoise and aquamarine. We're talking small spaces with bold bedspreads and curtains in these shocking color combos. Looking back, I feel bad for whoever had to try to sleep in those rooms.

I lived in a drab dorm room my first year at Syracuse but in my second year, to round out my college experience, I moved into a sorority. I'd always wanted to have the camaraderie of a group of girls. I thought living in a sorority house would feel like a close-knit family for me, but we sisters never felt all that connected. I did have a roommate whom I liked, a journalism major named Diane. We two were pretty much the outcasts in the house. I was still heavy and still overeating. And Diane was a real studious type with cat's eye glasses and problem hair. She and I used to raid the icebox at night and gorge ourselves in our room. When the house mother found out, she put a lock on the icebox door, so we started hoarding food in our room, which was strictly forbidden. I remember we would cleverly stuff pairs of pantyhose with all of our contraband and hang them out the window, just like Ray Milland did with his liquor bottles in *The Lost Weekend.*

One of my only memories of sorority life bonding was when the Beatles were on *The Ed Sullivan Show* for the first time. Our house mother called upstairs to us when the program was about to start, and we all came running down like thunder to claim our places on the couch, chairs, and floor. We all screamed along with the girls in the Ed Sullivan audience before the music even started. I had a major crush on Paul.

Another sorority memory I have was when President Kennedy was shot. All classes were canceled, and our whole house sat transfixed in front of the TV set for an entire day. I and all of my sisters actually cried on one another's shoulders.

My first year at Syracuse I joined the cheerleading squad, and by my second year I was named head cheerleader. That was a *huge* deal, as Syracuse was a major football school. As head cheerleader I got to travel with the team to the out-of-town games. They didn't send the whole squad—just me and the head male cheerleader. At the start of those games I was the one who had the honor of leading the team out onto the field. There's something very powerful about having an entire team of football players following you. You can actually *feel* it surging behind you. I would high-step with my thunder thighs and shake my pom-poms. Then I'd turn, face the team, and back flip off the field, signaling the start of the game.

Losing It

Throughout my college career I always dated the jocks. And it was all pretty innocent. In fact, nothing serious ever happened between me and a boy until my junior year when I made a momentous decision: I was finally going to go to bed with a boy. All of the other girls I knew had already made the leap, and I was feeling childishly left behind. I was curious to find out what all the hubbub was about.

My plan was to attend a football game at the campus of our nearest rival school, Colgate University, and to pick up one of the players. I wanted my first to be a guy from another campus because I didn't want to foul my own nest, as the saying goes.

I went with my roommate and one of the other cheerleaders, neither of whom had any idea about my ulterior motive. We planned to get rooms at a motel and stay overnight, and I made sure I got my own room. Since I didn't own anything remotely sexy or suggestive I had to borrow an outfit from another friend, a real Sandy Barker type. I still remember the outfit. It was a tight tweedy pencil skirt that came to just below the knee; very nubby, it looked like oatmeal with little yellow flecks in it. I topped it with a tight lacy blouse under which I wore what was known as a bullet bra, one of those satin conical things. Very Madonna, very Gaultier. It was actually a Maidenform bra, and while I was putting it on and stuffing it, I remembered those ads in the magazines and a line flashed through my head: *I dreamt I lost my virginity in my Maidenform bra.* I laughed out loud, which helped ease some of the anxiety I was feeling. I sat down and put on a pair of pointy-toed kitten heel shoes and I was ready to go.

We made the bumpy three-hour drive in my friend's battered Plymouth Valiant, which bucked when it started and smelled of diesel fuel. She had affectionately named the car Val. I was uncharacteristically quiet during the ride as I kept playing out the possible scenario in my head. I pictured it being like a fairy tale with the prince, wearing a football uniform, sweeping me off my feet and carrying me up the castle stairs. Slow fade and then cut! I didn't actually fantasize about the ultimate act itself.

When we arrived we went immediately to the game and, sitting in the bleachers, nervous yet determined, I started looking over the players. I settled on a good-looking guy who just happened to be the tight end. (No pun intended.) I watched him throughout the entire game and really liked his moves on the field and wondered how his moves were off the field. I was really ready to make this happen. I was ready to do it and get it over with.

After the game my girlfriends, who still had no idea about my scheme, and I went to a party at one of the frat houses. I'm sure they were wondering why I was so dolled up for a football game, but I managed to lose them pretty quickly and go in search of my tight end. When I spotted him across the room, I walked over to him and made some small talk. I complimented him on the game, which Colgate had won, and quickly asked him to come back to my motel with me. Well, I didn't have to ask him twice. Judging from where his eyes were, that bullet bra was doing the talking for me.

My room was appropriately tacky for what was about to happen, but it was all I could afford. It had plastic plants and plastic covering on the couch and chairs and smelled of stale cigarette smoke and pine-scented air freshener. The floral bedspread was stained, as was the carpet, framed pictures of puppies and kittens decorated the walls. The only window looked out depressingly over the parking lot. Hardly the castle I had imagined.

Now, I'm a girl who likes a little romance and I was way out of my comfort zone so I just let him take the lead. I won't go into detail here, but we took care of business, and I was extremely disappointed. Classic, right? I think I had built up the whole notion of sex so much in my mind and made it into such a big deal that how could it have been anything but a disappointment? It wasn't the boy's fault. He was nice enough, but I made him leave shortly after.

As disappointing as the act itself was, I did feel an enormous amount of relief. I had done it. I felt as if I had just joined a special kind of club. When I walked out of the motel alone the next morning—and it may have been the kitten heels—I swear, I felt a few inches taller. I was a woman.

3.) I NEVER GOT MY GARDENIA.

I'd always loved *Mademoiselle* magazine and by the time I got to college I read it religiously. It had a sexy, kind of Frenchy *yé-yé* feel that made it different from the other fashion magazines in the early 1960s. It also featured great stories by up-and-coming writers. I'd skim them from time to time but I wasn't really into literature. I was always more turned on by anything visual and I loved *Mademoiselle*'s layouts. It referred to itself as "a quality magazine for smart young women." It was the fashion magazine with a *brain*.

In 1963, at the beginning of my senior year at Syracuse, I saw an announcement in *Mademoiselle* for a contest that would celebrate the best that young America had to offer. It sounded like

the answer to a prayer. The winners of the contest would spend a month in New York City as guest editors working on the September issue of the magazine—"The College Issue," as it was known. The winners would also be treated to one week of travel to a foreign country as youth ambassadors. The contest was open to any college girls interested in fashion, art, and writing. You'll notice I said "girls." The contest had always been open only to girls, but sometime in the late seventies, the magazine broadened its horizons to include boys as well.

My mind was racing. I didn't actually know *what* I wanted to do after I graduated. All I knew is that I had to get back to New York City to do it, and this contest could be my chance. I didn't think twice before filling out the application and sending it in, along with examples of my artwork, which at the time were mostly abstract sketches, some watercolors, and portraits of my friends and members of my family.

In about a week I received a letter saying that my application had been accepted, and I was in the running to be one of twenty girls picked to be guest editor. One of twenty—those weren't impossible odds. I didn't take into account how many thousands of applicants there must have been. The letter also explained that the selection process would take a year and that I'd be sent assignments once a month. These would include essays, illustrations, design ideas—that sort of thing. What they were really doing was trying to find out what was on girls' minds, to pick our brains; a very smart marketing strategy.

I went to the library and did a little research and learned that it was actually a very prestigious contest and a win would put me in some pretty good company. Among the previous winners were Sylvia Plath, Joan Didion, and Candice Bergen. I was now even more determined to win.

I entered the contest in October, and each month of my senior year I looked forward to receiving the next assignment to inspire me. Sure, it meant I had to find time in my already heavy workload to do them, but I didn't care. Every new exercise I completed meant I was closer to the finish line, winning the contest, and living in New York City. It wasn't that I was overconfident. All I knew is that I *wanted* it more than anything I had ever wanted in my life.

At this point in my schooling, I wasn't interested in fashion. I was too laser focused on art. But seeing as I already knew how to cut and sew from helping my mom with my dancing costumes when I was little, it was inevitable that my illustrations and fabric designs would spill over to sewing projects, and I started to make clothing for myself using the fabrics I had printed. It was a completely natural progression.

I didn't make anything too fancy or difficult. The pieces were all easy-peasy: a tank dress with a scoop neck or an A-line shift. Looking back, they were very Mary Quant. The shape worked for me—Twiggy flat on top and thunder thighs on the bottom. The dresses had very few seams, no darts, and no embellishments. They didn't need any complications, since the prints were crazy enough. Back then my clothes rarely even had a zipper, which in retrospect I realize was pretty radical. In the early sixties we were coming off that old structured shape that dominated fashion since the end of World War II. That silhouette made women look very phony baloney, all padded hips and cone bras, stiff clothes and panty girdles. They were the Spanx of their day. My much simpler design suited both my tastes and my sewing skills.

Finally, just before graduation, a telegram arrived. I'll never forget how I felt receiving it and I've saved it to this day. A Western Union guy came to the door of my sorority house and said, "Telegram for Miss Betsey Johnson." It was just like in the movies. I said, "I'm Betsey Johnson," and he handed me an envelope. I gave him a quarter tip and took a deep breath.

I said to myself, *Okay, Betsey, either your parents are dead or you won the contest.* I opened the envelope and let out a sigh. Sure enough, Mom and Dad were safe. I'd won!

I started screaming and jumping up and down, but there was no one there to hear me. I was all alone in the house. Even if there had been someone else at home, she wouldn't have known what all the fuss was about. I hadn't shared my entry in the contest with any of my sorority sisters. I'm superstitious by nature and I didn't want to jinx myself. Besides, they wouldn't have understood why I wanted to enter this kind of competition in the first place. The girls in my sorority were the other cheerleaders, not my art-class sisters.

I read the first line over and over to make sure I was reading it correctly, that there was no mistake. When I had convinced myself that it wasn't just wishful thinking, I read the rest of the telegram. The date I was told to report to work in New York City meant I would miss my own college graduation.

I knew at that instant that I was okay with that. As much as I had loved and enjoyed college life, I didn't need a long, boring graduation ceremony. I was done with this prep phase of my life and more than ready to move up and on.

I immediately placed a rare long-distance person-to-person call to my mother to tell her the news. She screamed and jumped up and down, too. She knew how much the contest meant to me. I had taken the risk and shared the secret with her early on during one of our weekly phone calls. Since then Mom had called me once a week like clockwork to check in with my progress.

Miss Johnson wins fashion editing post on Mademoiselle

Betsey Johnson, a vivacious and talented Syracuse University senior, is one of 20 young women who have won a competition to be guest editors of Mademoiselle this year.

Miss Johnson, 21, the daughter of Mr. and Mrs. J. Herman Johnson of 214 Wolcott Hill Rd., Wethersfield, will spend a month as a paid member of the editorial staff of Mademoiselle. She will help edit the August "Passport to

MISS BETSEY JOHNSON
(WHS PHOTO, 1960)

Campus" issue. The prizes also include a trip to Britain, with visits to Edin-

burgh, London, Stratford, and Oxford.

An All-round student at Syracuse, the petite, brown-haired Miss Johnson was cited at last week's Honors convocation for "excellence in the creative arts," having placed first in the senior class in he School of Art. She has also been a cheer leader and a member of several honorary societies.

Miss Johnson's winning entries included designs for party costumes, a formal dress, and a fabric for drapes which has already been chosen for use at the university in a wo-

men's dormitory.

She also wrote and illustrated an experimental children's book which incorporates textures such as a sponge and sandpaper for the child to touch. Miss Johnson will be taking the book to New York with her in hopes of finding a publisher.

The local paper announcing my Mademoiselle *win. Thanks, Mom, for saving this.*

Two weeks later my parents made the four-hour drive from Terryville to Syracuse to collect me and my three years of college stuff to bring back home for the shortest of visits.

I spent that week at home furiously trying to pull myself together for my new life in New York City. *Mademoiselle* still hadn't told us to what country or even continent they would be sending us guest editors. I did remember seeing in the magazine the previous year, the girls had gone to Russia, which back then was pretty heavy going, so I realized that anywhere was possible. I didn't know what to pack, but I had faith. I figured if they were sending us somewhere crazy like Siberia they would have told us to bring a heavy coat and long underwear.

With my mother's help, I made a few more dresses from the fabrics that I had printed in school. *Mademoiselle* told us that our daytime wardrobe would be provided for us by various clothing manufacturers who advertised in the magazine. These were the outfits we'd be required to wear for photo shoots and appearances we'd be making. But what we wore on our downtime would be up to us, and I wanted to look the part of the bright young thing.

The day finally came for my trip to my new life in New York City, and I could hardly contain myself. I didn't sleep a wink the night before and woke my parents at the crack of dawn, just as if it were Christmas.

From Connecticut, we drove straight to the Barbizon Hotel for Women on Sixty-Third Street, which would be our home base. My parents were assured that we would be heavily chaperoned. They needn't have worried. The Barbizon was like a fortress. There were signs all over the place: No Men Allowed! It was all very uptown and white gloves, a very ladylike, straight-arrow type of place. After my parents made sure I was settled in, they hightailed it out of town as fast as my father's new Chevy could take them.

We had all of one afternoon to unpack and get acquainted. All of us girls were bound by our mutual excitement and got along like a house on fire. We knew that we were a very special bunch. They assigned us two to a room, and we must have sounded like a pack of hens the way we were all yakking. The girls were from all over the country and were so interesting. We were split right down the middle, half journalism majors and half art majors.

We would find out the following day which department at the magazine we'd be working in. I was, of course, hoping to be assigned to the editorial art department, but so were a lot of the girls. That night there was an informal dinner in the Barbizon dining hall, where we would have most of our meals, and then we were told we had to be in bed early. We may have been in New York City and we may have felt more or less on our own, but we weren't really independent.

They weren't kidding: the next morning we were awakened at six a.m. I showered and dressed in a kind of dream state. We hadn't yet been given our assigned outfits from our sponsors, so we were free to wear what we liked. As we ran out the door I looked around, and every one of us was dressed to impress. But not in the same way. The sixties look hadn't really come on strong yet, and a lot of the girls looked as if they were still stuck in the 1950s. I chose one of my more subdued patterned A-line dresses, but I still kind of stuck out. I also wore a new pair of yellow stack-heeled Mary Janes I had bought just for the trip. I should have broken them in first. They pinched my feet all day.

We walked eight blocks downtown as one large group. It was one of those perfect late spring days, with a warm breeze blowing and not a cloud in the sky. As we headed south on Park Avenue it looked like the whole city was in bloom. There was a garden of multicolored flowers planted straight down the middle of the street as far as the eye could see. I just loved it, but this beautiful sight was lost on the hundreds of people who all seemed to be walking in the opposite direction with their heads down rushing to work.

When we reached the magazine offices, there was the standard meet and greet over breakfast, but I could hardly touch my food because I was so excited to receive my assignment. When breakfast was done and the food cleared away, all of the editors lined up at the front of the room, and we were introduced to Edie Locke, the fashion editor, who was running the show. A rolling rack was then wheeled in, and we got to see the first outfit that we would be photographed wearing later in the day.

There were twenty garment bags on the rack, each with one of our names on it. A few weeks earlier we had had to provide the magazine with a very detailed list of our measurements. (I wasn't happy with mine.) I just hoped the outfits would be as flattering on me as my own were. I knew how to dress for my figure. Every one of us twenty girls was a different shape and size, so not everything was going to look good on everybody.

We all went up and found our garment bag and unzipped it, and out popped twenty identical outfits: a double-breasted, houndstooth pattern jacket, a matching knee-length pleated skirt, a rib-knit turtleneck sweater, and a black beret. And we were expected to wear black-and-white saddle shoes and white kneesocks. I was miserable. This getup was going to make me look like a cow.

They then finally announced our assignments. More bad news: I'd be placed in the fabric department. Yes, it sounds strange now, but *Mademoiselle*—and in fact, most of the women's magazines—had a section dedicated to fabrics. This was a place where you could find out about new textiles and in some cases even get free patterns. People still did a lot of home sewing back then, and all of the major stores had fabric departments as well.

I was bummed out. This assignment was not at all what I wanted. Remember, the only reason I had even taken the fabric design class was to support my illustrating. Compared to all the other departments at the magazine, this one sounded as dull as dishwater. I tried to mask my disappointment and stayed focused on the larger and more important picture—basically living the dream. I thought to myself, *Okay, Betsey, get a grip. Put on a happy face and just do the best job you can.* If nothing else, I was a trouper.

My editor was a woman named D. J. White. The first thing I noticed about her was that she was very, very pregnant. She looked uncomfortable and as if she was about to burst at any moment, but she was full of energy and enthusiasm and seemed very glad to have me on board. She took me by the hand and said, "Oh, Betsey! We are going to have fun!" Then she told me she loved my dress and was genuinely impressed when I told her that I made it.

As unenthusiastic as I was about the fabric department, I quickly became very enthusiastic about D.J. Even on that first day I saw how positively people reacted to her. I especially noticed that she could get *anybody* excited about *anything.* She was an absolute, natural-born cheerleader, a quality I could certainly appreciate.

D.J. explained that I would be spending each day working with her. That is, when we weren't being dragged all over town for photo shoots—and before we were sent to Russia, or wherever. There would be at least one photo op a day, mostly posing around the city at famous landmarks—hanging off the Staten Island Ferry, walking through Central Park, riding a carousel at Coney Island, all the usual touristy things. All twenty of us in matching outfits provided by the good people at Crazy

Horse or Cacharel or whatever other label was looking for some free press. We did everything but form a human pyramid in Times Square! It was fun at first, but quickly became tedious and tiring.

But when I was with D.J., I was excited. Her enthusiasm was absolutely infectious. She brought me along to all of her appointments with fabric companies. And she wasn't just into fashion. We met with people who were making upholstery for car seats, and not only car seats but for seats on *rocket ships*! Back then, there was always a lot of talk about getting to the moon.

One afternoon, during my first week at the magazine, D.J. said to me, "Find out where the New York Yankees buy the pinstriped fabric for their uniforms. Call 'em up!" And I did. I discovered who supplied the fabric, and she wrote about it in the magazine. I don't know who would have been interested in that subject, but I was fascinated—not with Yankee uniforms, but with D.J.'s thought process. She always thought way outside the box and always unconventionally. She taught me, for example, how to use fabrics for something other than their intended use. When we got a sample of the car seat upholstery, I remember her looking at it, handling it for a while, and then, seemingly out of nowhere, saying, "Ya know, this would make a *fabulous* coat." This way of thinking stayed with me for the rest of my career. I owe D.J. a huge debt of gratitude for that.

After a week into the guest editorship, the magazine held a dinner to announce where our big trip would take us. When we walked into the conference room where the dinner was being served, it was decked out in Union Jacks, and the menu included Beef Wellington. It didn't take a genius to figure out that we were heading to London. I think I actually screamed.

London! This was like another dream come true. In 1963 you could not *possibly* be going anywhere more exciting. This was the London of mods and rockers, Mary Quant and miniskirts, Carnaby Street and Vidal Sassoon. It was absolute ground zero for cool, and I couldn't wait to be part of it.

London

When it was finally time to go to the airport, I realized that I had never been on an airplane. I hadn't thought about the actual flight until that very moment, as I'd been too excited fantasizing about London. As a matter of fact, until I went to Pratt as a freshman, I had never been out of New England. I was terrified to fly but also curious.

A van took us out to the recently renamed Kennedy Airport, where we posed for more photographs inside the Pan Am terminal wearing our matching red, white, and blue designer schoolgirl outfits—again, with kneesocks. (The magazine *really* pushed the wholesome college girl image.)

When we boarded the plane, I was struck by how small it felt and I realized that I would be in a tin can for seven hours flying over nothing but water. It was only the excitement of all of my magazine sorority sisters that kept me from freaking out. We ended up spending the entire seven hours yakking nonstop.

When we finally landed we boarded a private tour bus that would take us to the Hilton Hyde Park Hotel. Once we hit the city, I looked out the windows with wide eyes taking it all in. I thought London looked a lot like New York City, but older, and it certainly didn't seem as foreign as I thought it would be.

But it was the people who really caught my eye. If I thought New Yorkers were sophisticated and had their looks pulled together, Londoners were a whole different ball game. People were actually dressed like the models I'd seen in magazines. Girls really *did* wear white lipstick, skirts really *were* that short, men really *did* wear crazy-colored suits. And boy, were they cute with their mod haircuts. London was the first place I ever saw silver fabric, and it left an indelible mark on me. People looked like *aliens*, and I loved it! Sitting there on the bus and looking out the window, I suddenly felt like a country bumpkin, even in my wild floral minidress.

Before any more sightseeing, we had to listen to a lecture. Edie Locke had come with us and laid down the law. She told us that our nine a.m. to nine p.m. duties in London would be similar to those in New York. There would be luncheons and cocktail parties and, of course, more photos. This trip was *not* meant to be a vacation.

Edie then introduced us to Murray, a photographer *Made-*

moiselle had hired to shoot our pictures. He was to go everywhere with us for the entire week. He was tall and very thin and had a mop of sandy-colored hair. Of course, I managed to fall for him. Very innocently, mind you, but his attention and mild flirtations added just one more fairy-tale element to the trip.

The dinner parties usually ended at nine, after which our time was our own to do whatever we wished. The only problem was that we were usually so exhausted after a long day promoting the magazine that we just wanted to go back to the boring old Hilton and crash.

We all hated to go against Edie, for whom we had so much respect, but the lure of London nightlife was too much to resist. We snuck out. It wasn't hard to do as there was much less of a watchful eye here than at the steel-trap Barbizon. Besides, Edie was completely conked out in her room.

True, we *were* exhausted, but fortunately one of the girls had a bottle of little pink pills that she assured us would keep us up all night. And they did.

Left to our own devices we would have had no idea what to do with ourselves or where to go. But thanks to Murray, we had our own personal guide to London nightlife. He took us to a lot of underground clubs. And I mean *literally* underground. We always seemed to be going down some narrow stairs into a loud, dark space. Many of them had mattresses on the floor. I don't know if they were for encouraging sleeping or sex. Due to the pink pills, none of us was in the mood for either. But boy did we dance! I think I got only two hours of sleep each night during that week.

On our third day we made a trip out of the city to Stratford-upon-Avon, Shakespeare land. Predictably decked out in tweed and little tams, we frolicked in the English midsummer sun while Murray snapped away. I hated leaving London even for just a one-day trip as I felt as if I was missing something. This country scene just reminded me of Connecticut. I was more interested in life in the city and don't remember much about good old Stratford except for seeing a lot of thatched roofs and everyone picking hay out of their hair.

At the end of the week there was a formal dinner party hosted by Marietta Tree. Mrs. Tree, as we were instructed to call her, was the head of a very rich and influential Boston family and was named some kind of cultural ambassador to England. I guess the magazine thought she would give our last dinner in London just the right classy tone. Coincidentally, Marietta Tree was also the mother of sixties supermodel Penelope Tree, who in 1966 I would dress for Truman Capote's Black and White Ball.

Due to our early-morning flight to New York, none of us went out the last night in London.

This time I didn't have the energy to be scared of flying. All of us girls passed out practically as soon as we took off.

Hitting the Ground Running

After the magic of London, it may have been back to New York, but it was hardly back to Earth. We had only a couple of weeks to prepare the college issue, and I was nervously anticipating what *that* kind of pressure would be like.

When, still groggy from the flight, I walked through the door on my first day back, I was greeted by D.J.'s assistant, Mary, who was frantic. D.J., who was long overdue to give birth, had finally popped the day after we left for London and she was out on maternity leave. It was up to me and Mary to finish her column about the rocket ship seat covers and turn it in on time. Talk about on-the-job training! I actually had to place some fact-checking calls to NASA.

With D.J. out on leave, Edie Locke became my mentor. She had a bubbly personality that you could not possibly be unhappy around. She took me under her wing and helped make that final week of the guest editorship so much fun. When our column was safely put to bed, Edie called me into her office. I thought I had made some fatal error, botched the thread count on the seat covers or something. But instead she offered me a fill-in position at the magazine while D.J. was on leave. Edie had noticed and been impressed with how fast I caught on around the office and with my behavior in London. (She had no idea about the little pink pep pills.) I was just blown away. This was working out better than if I had planned it all out myself, which I hadn't, not by a long shot. I just went with the flow.

I was now a full-fledged member of the art department—a very junior member, mind you. Be that as it may, I thought, *Hey, this is my big chance!* What I wound up doing was answering the phones, routing photostats between departments, and viewing portfolios from artists and photographers. It may sound boring, but it wasn't. I took every job, big or small, that they would throw at me. It was great because I never got locked into doing just one thing. This way I not only met and interacted with everyone in my own department, but with other departments as well. In the process I really learned how a magazine is run. I remember getting so energized by the electric atmosphere of the office. The air just hummed and buzzed.

When I had to deliver papers to the steno pool, I couldn't hear myself think for the clacking of the typewriters. It was like a scene right out of one of my favorite movies, *Funny Face*, starring Audrey Hepburn. As a matter of fact, the editor in chief, Betsy Blackwell, could have been the prototype for the Kay Thompson character in that film. You remember: Think pink! I found her *completely* intimidating. Luckily, I was reporting directly to Edie Locke, who never played the role of the grand fashion maven but treated me more like a sister.

Now that I was a full-time employee, it was time to say goodbye to the Barbizon, which, even with all of its rules, I had come to love. It represented such a turning point in my life, and

I felt grown-up there. I was on the lookout for another living situation, which my parents *insisted* be another female-only hotel. I eventually found a place downtown on Eleventh Street between Fifth and Sixth avenues, which was a much hipper area than the Barbizon's buttoned-up Midtown neighborhood. The house was run by a very severe-looking older woman. Thinking back, she was probably only forty. But she was matronly looking with an outdated Gibson girl hairdo and skirts all the way to the ground. She was *very* serious about her rules. Slip up once and you were out, she informed me when I first went to look at the room. She was also fond of referring to the other tenants fondly as her "girls," as in *"My* girls are well behaved." I remember thinking, *What year is this?* Her name, believe it or not, was Mrs. Stern.

I could hardly wrap my head around the rule about curfew. All residents had to be in their rooms and accounted for by eleven p.m. or be locked out for the night. I couldn't believe it. This was New York City, the city that never sleeps. This did not bode well for me as I had just started dating one of the fake Beatles from the World's Fair, which had just opened out in Flushing, Queens.

Practically every day, as soon as I finished at the magazine, I and some of the other girls would rush out to the fairgrounds to see the not really Beatles play. Their last set didn't end until after nine, and then we had to take the subway all the way back to the city. More often than not I'd arrive late to the residence only to find the doors locked and I would have to find some fleabag hotel for the night. The next day I'd offer up some phoney-baloney excuse to the matron, who, unbelievably, fell for it. Maybe she wasn't so severe after all.

I spoke too soon. I ended up getting thrown out for smoking. One of the maids found an ashtray with just one cigarette in it on my windowsill, but apparently that was enough.

I didn't know what I was going to do. While I had a full-time job at the magazine, it paid very little. I knew I did *not* want to get a roommate. I'd had enough of that at college and at the Barbizon. I was twenty-one years old and knew it was time to be on my own. As luck would have it, one of the girls at the magazine knew someone who was giving up her place. It was a fifth-floor walk-up railroad apartment in Brooklyn. In fact, it was directly under the Brooklyn Bridge. Though the rent was pretty low, on my salary it would still be tight, but I figured out a way to swing it: I started making little tops, hoping to sell them to the girls around the office as a way to supplement my income.

I found this hand-crocheted-looking fabric at one of the markets that D.J. had introduced me to. I cut and sewed it into sweaters that hugged the body. They had short, tight sleeves and a scoop neck that was trimmed with half-inch velvet. I finished them off with a little bow on the front.

They were adorable, if I do say so myself. I wore one of them to work and got plenty of compliments on it. When the girls found out I made the sweater myself, they started asking me to make more, for them. I got my dad to lend me the money to buy three hundred yards of the crocheted fabric. In no time at all I had a bunch of orders, and at twenty dollars a pop, I was able to pay him back right away.

I made a poster with an illustration of a girl wearing the sweater and hung it up in the ladies' room at the magazine. Well, that did it. It seemed as if every girl at *Mademoiselle* wanted one. I even began branching out and copying some of the dresses I had made for myself. My efforts must have impressed some of the higher-ups, because they asked to shoot one of the sweaters on a model and feature it in the "Shop Here" section of the magazine. This was a *huge* deal for me. But be careful what you wish for.

Once the picture ran in the magazine the orders *really* started to fly in. I was still making the tops by hand, one at a time. Every day after work I would climb those five flights of stairs and stay up until one in the morning cutting and sewing. As grueling as this might sound, I loved it and knew I had discovered what I really wanted to do.

One of the first orders I received soon after the top was featured in the magazine was from Kim Novak. Yes, *the* Kim Novak, one of my favorite actresses. I loved her in *Picnic* and *Bell, Book and Candle*. I even felt a bit of a connection to her, as my dear Ann Pimm had been in *Pal Joey* on Broadway in the same role that Kim Novak had played in the movie. And now she wanted one of my sweaters! I had shipped lots of orders, but this one made it all very real. For the first time I realized that my clothes were out there in the world and people were wearing them.

When I shipped her the sweater, I tucked a handwritten thank-you card into the box. It read "Dear Kim Novak, thank you for buying my sweater!! XOX Betsey." She sent *me* back a note, along with an order for two more.

This experience taught me a very good lesson in customer service, something that I put into practice for my entire design career: My clothes would always include a hang tag with a printed note from me.

Life was good. I had my own apartment, a job that I loved, and a thriving mail-order business that enabled me to discover something that I loved doing—even if it did take up all of my spare time. By now I'd been at *Mademoiselle* long enough to learn about a wonderful, sort of old-fashioned tradition they had of rewarding employees with a gardenia after one year of service. I didn't last the entire year—only nine months, to be exact—so I never did get my gardenia. But that was okay. One flower was a small price to pay for what Edie Locke was about to do for me.

4.) CLOTHING TO WEAR ON THE MOON: PARAPHERNALIA.

E die had heard some buzz within the industry that Puritan Fashions, a huge clothing manufacturer, was backing a new store slated to open in a few months. The store was going to be called Paraphernalia, which was a boutique concept very popular in London started by a visionary young man named Paul Young.

Paul's idea was to set up individual shops within big department stores to give a stable of up-and-coming designers such as Foale and Tuffin, Daniel Hechter, Emanuel Kahn, and Paco Rabanne a platform to sell clothes the likes of which people hadn't seen before. It was all new, new, new! This is the model used now in all department stores, but Paul was the man who invented it. He was a retail genius and was even responsible for introducing Mary Quant to the American market during his brief stint at J. C. Penney.

Karl Rosen, the man who owned Puritan Fashions, lured Paul to New York City, in hopes that he could work the same magic there. Paul's specific vision for New York was to cater to young, rich-girl society types and bring downtown uptown. And it wasn't just for girls: boys could shop there, too . . . as long as they were skinny enough and didn't mind their buttons and flies on the wrong side.

I had been working for *Mademoiselle* for nine months when on a Friday morning, Edie approached me to say that Paul had called her asking for names of interesting new designers. I wondered what this had to do with me. *I* wasn't a designer, I just made clothes for the girls around the office and for my mail-order gig, but a *real* designer . . . me? Uh-uh. I certainly didn't think of myself that way.

She went on to say that she had set up a meeting for me with Paul on the following Monday afternoon. I was shocked and told her, "But that only gives me the weekend to pull it together!"

"Oh," she replied calmly, "I'm sure you can handle it."

I didn't know what to do first. I was already staying up until all hours working to keep up with my orders. How was I supposed to make anything new to show Paul!?

I had no time to waste, so I ran around the office and talked to every girl who had bought something from me. By then I had graduated from making the little crocheted tops to super-simple stretchy little dresses as well. I asked them to bring the clothes they had bought to the office on Monday morning so I could borrow them back for my interview. They were all excited for me and more than happy to help.

When I got home that night, I gathered up all the stuff I had made for myself and was kind of amazed at the amount of clothes. Maybe Edie was on to something. Maybe I *was* a designer.

I spent the entire weekend redrawing sketches of all the clothing I had made and did new sketches of things I planned to make, all done in crayon, which is how I always worked.

As you can imagine, the weekend passed in a blur. I think I might have slept as much as two hours each night, if I slept at all.

When I got to the office on Monday morning, all the girls whom I had asked to bring in clothes came by and dropped them off at the art department. I'd fold each dress or whatever the garment was neatly and add it to one of the suitcases I had brought in to lug them to Paul's office.

When lunchtime arrived I was out the door like a shot to make my way to 1400 Broadway, the address Edie had given me. When I ran into her on my way out, she said, "I'd wish you luck, but you don't need it." Buoyed by her confidence, I briskly walked all the way to the Puritan offices.

It was an unusually hot day for so early in the summer, and

I was sweating when I finally reached my destination. I was wearing one of the dresses I had made myself. It was short but not too short—that would come later. It was also brightly colored but not too bright—that would come later as well. It wasn't at all crazy, like some of the sketches I had done. I thought it was better to err on the side of conservative . . . or at least my version of what conservative was.

I had just had my hair cut in the Vidal Sassoon style. Not that I could afford to have my hair cut at the salon. I was actually dating a hairdresser from Sassoon who gave me the haircut at his apartment. I remember he used his chrome toaster instead of a mirror to see how he was doing. With my outfit and new do, I thought I was looking every inch the savvy New York designer.

I gazed up at the tall building smack-dab in the middle of the Garment District. Edie had told me that Puritan owned the entire building as well as other buildings in the area. I think she wanted to impress upon me just how huge an organization it was. But I was more intimidated than impressed and wondered again if I really could work as a fashion designer. As intimidating as that possibility was, it was also exciting. It had been quite the crazy year. First the contest, then the eye-opening trip to London, the job at *Mademoiselle,* and now this interview. I must have had more than one lucky star shining down on me.

I tried not to place too much importance on the interview. I told myself to just do my best and go with the flow. Whatever happens, happens. If it didn't work out, I'd still have my job at the magazine. Coming back to the moment, I put any negative thoughts out of my head and, holding tightly on to my two hard Samsonite suitcases, strode into the building with as much confidence as I could fake.

When I got up to the twelfth floor, where I had been instructed to meet Paul, I saw that it was an old, run-of-the-mill kind of office, a little shabby even, which surprised me, as I had expected something fancy, stylish, and chic. Oh, boy, did I have a lot to learn about the garment business!

Out of nowhere appeared a secretary, as unglamorous as the office, who led me all the way to the back of the huge, crowded space. I was further surprised to see that this big shot didn't even have a real office, just a desk and a couple of chairs tucked into a corner between what looked like a mile of rolling racks.

I walked up to his desk and, with my nerves jumping all over the place, said as brightly as I could, "Hi! I'm Betsey." He looked up from what he was doing, and I saw that he was a good-looking, very unbusinesslike Englishman in his early thirties. But what made more of an impression on me was what he was doing. He had piles of paper on his desk and he was doodling . . . *in colored crayon!* I felt a connection immediately.

He smiled at me and said, "Edie spoke very highly of you, and I've been looking forward to meeting you. Why don't you show me what you've got."

I heaved my heavy suitcases onto his desk and when I popped them open they practically exploded. Paul started to go through my things, slowly and hesitant at first, and then more quickly. I convinced myself that he was trying to get through it all in a hurry before asking me to leave. He was completely silent the whole time as I absentmindedly bit my nails.

Finally, after scrutinizing my last drawing, he collapsed exhaustedly into his desk chair, looked up at me, smiled, and said, "When can you start?"

I almost asked "When can I start *what?*" before I realized what he meant. I was in shock. Just like that he had decided that I was going to be Paraphernalia's newest designer.

I would later learn that that was the way it was done. Paul's word was law. He said either yes or no, and that was it. He knew instinctively if something was going to work. There was no long approval process for anything.

When my initial shock wore off, we got down to business. He told me that his plan was to open Paraphernalia in three months and that all of my clothes would have to be delivered by then.

I would be responsible for the design and I was expected to produce the first sample. The Paraphernalia people would be responsible for the actual production, getting my designs into factories and produced. They'd decide how many of each garment would be made, organize deliveries, and so on and so on. Thank God! I would have had no idea how any of that worked.

Then, best of all, he told me that my name would be on the

label. It was to read "Designed by Betsey Johnson for Para-phernalia."

At the time I didn't have a clue how special and unusual a thing it is to have your name on a label and I want to point this out to all of you design students out there: *this is not how it usually works!* People slave for years before their name goes on a label.

I wasn't going to be the only designer. Paul told me he had already hired a few others, and I was dying to meet them. There was a girl named Deanna Litell, who was already kind of established. Her clothes were very bold, very graphic. Lots of black-and-white pieces. The others were Michael Mott, with his military-style clothes, and Diana Dew, who did fabulous electric dresses. Another designer, Joel Schumacher, was only making capes. Incidentally, if this name sounds familiar, it should. This is the same Joel Schumacher who went on to become famous for directing the movies *Batman Forever, St. Elmo's Fire,* and *The Lost Boys,* to name a few.

Paul went on to explain that I would receive very little help from the Paraphernalia organization . . . whatever that actually was. Paul was the only person I was in contact with, and even that contact was spotty. I was to be paid a salary. I don't recall how much, exactly, but it must have been decent, because I was able to afford a larger apartment.

They did set me up with a small workroom in another one of the Puritan buildings and hired me a pattern maker. She was a beautiful hippie-dippie Greek girl named Tulah, who ended up working with me off and on for most of the rest of my career. And thank God for that. Until then I had been winging it— doing patterns my own way, which worked because my dresses at that time were very simple. I'd lie down on the floor on top of the pattern paper and just trace my own body with a crayon. Real pattern making is actually a quite specific skill, and very tricky. You begin by looking at a fashion illustration and interpreting what each of the lines and curves means. You apply these interpretations to a sheet of thin tissue paper and come up with a series of shapes that you cut out, and then you move onto pattern paper, which is more substantial. *Then*, and only then, do

Typical me! On the floor in my Paraphernalia workroom.

A trio of my Paraphernalia looks

you trace the pattern pieces onto the actual fabric you'll be using. Whew! I was glad I was going to have someone doing it for me.

After spending eight hours in the workroom, most days Tulah and I would continue making the patterns at my apartment at night. I was expected to pay for my samples myself, out of pocket, and get reimbursed later, which I thought was a little odd. In fact, the way they handled the whole business side of things seemed strange. But what did I know? I had nothing to compare it to. I just assumed that was how the garment business was run.

As far as meeting the other designers, I never even saw them, as we were all working in separate locations. Paraphernalia wasn't run like a big creative lab, but just encouraged each of us to do our *own* thing. Do what we loved and what we were good at, and maybe keeping us apart was Paul's way of making sure that each of us did just that. More than likely, judging from Paul's "office" situation, they just stuck each of us wherever they had the space. I did meet Joel Schumacher once when he stopped by my place to pick up some fabric or something or other from me. All I ever remember Joel making was flamboyant capes.

Without any input from the powers that be, I had to figure out for myself how to get things done. I did reach out to D.J., and with her help I sourced lots of different kinds of fabrics; I designed one dress I called "Silverfish." It was a basic shift shape made out of silver lamé fishnet. I also found a great faux suede out of which I made something I called my "Story of O" dress. It was a little A-line with large, strategically placed brass grommets sewn into it, exposing your skin underneath.

These would all go on to be hugely popular and great sellers. They even inspired a brilliant ad campaign that included taglines like "Do you dare wear Betsey's Story of O dress?" or "Do you Silverfish?" But my favorite ad was one that was headlined "Are You Confused Enough for Paraphernalia?" It listed about a dozen insane questions. My favorites were:

"Are you getting obsessively caught up in your Dynel hairpieces?"

The "Story of O" dress and me already doing my splits

"Can you bear the strange din of your Betsey Johnson noise dress?"

"Are you discovering a new crueler you when you wear leather, nail-heads and aluminum?"

"Do you think A Dandy in Aspic should become a summer dish?"

The ads were so hysterical and groundbreaking and so quintessentially sixties. I don't know who came up with the concept, but Paul Young had the genius to find him or her.

Another early piece I did was something I called the "Julie Christie" dress, which was just my basic T-shirt design to which I added a starched collar and cuffs and little buttons up the front. It wasn't originally called the Julie Christie, but I dubbed it that when she wore it on the cover of *Mademoiselle* after she had won the Oscar for her role in the movie *Darling.* This was huge exposure for me. Julie Christie was *the* It girl of the moment. The magazine had brought in clothes from a whole bunch of designers, and she chose mine.

The Julie Christie gig wasn't a fluke. Paul had lots of Hollywood connections as well as New York society ones. In fact, to me it seemed as if there was no one he didn't know. He even got the French actress Anouk Aimée to ditch the Chanel outfits she was so famous for wearing and switch to mine. Not too shabby! Paul had a way of putting his connections to work . . . literally. He had the genius idea to hire Susan Burden as the store's manager. Susan was a well-known socialite and good friends with Joan Kennedy, so there were also intriguing political ties.

For the opening of Paraphernalia, I really didn't have a specific plan. I designed a ton of stuff, but there was no cohesive collection, no color story, no theme. All of my pieces were random one-offs. They were things I loved and believed in and wore myself. And Paul was fine with that.

I had done all of my design work months earlier, made the patterns, and produced the samples, which I handed over to one of Paul's people to do with what they would, and before I knew it the three months of waiting had flown by. I couldn't wait to see my designs all in a row on a rack in a store.

Just three days before the opening I got a call from Paul, which was unusual as I hadn't had much contact with him at all. I'd mostly been dealing with his production people. He sounded upset, and I figured it must be the stress as he was probably going nuts gearing up for what was going to be quite the unique store opening. Paul had taken me on a tour of the unfinished space just one week earlier, and even in its unfinished state I could tell it was going to be unlike any other store people had seen before. It was a big, stark white box with lots of mirrored surfaces and chrome. It was like stepping onto a spaceship or into the future. It was on Madison Avenue at Sixty-Seventh Street, strategically located right next door to Vidal Sassoon—another brilliant move on the part of Paul. He figured after a girl got her hair done she'd want to complete her new look with a new outfit.

I was about to find out that Paul wasn't suffering from pre-opening jitters. He laid it on me right away: "Betsey, something got screwed up at the factories. Your clothes will not be ready for the opening. I'm so sorry." I couldn't believe it. I had worked really hard and been so looking forward to the big night, and now this. The wind was knocked right out of my sails. I felt as if I had just been punched in the stomach.

Then he asked me if I had anything that I could get into the store. I swallowed hard, not wanting him to know how upset I was. I told him that I had some stuff and that in the next few days I could make a few more pieces. He said something like "Good girl!! I knew I could count on you." And that made me feel a little better . . . not much, but a little.

When the big night of the opening arrived—September 16, 1965, to be exact—I toyed with the idea of not going. I figured I could use the excuse of my clothes not arriving on time, which was true enough, but the real reason I didn't want to go was that I couldn't imagine being in the same room as all of the beautiful models who had been invited. There was talk that even Twiggy was going to be there! I felt that I was way too heavy to be standing next to these types of girls. Also, in spite of my chic Sassoon haircut, I never did quite convince myself that I passed for a hip young fashion designer. I assumed that the other designers for Paraphernalia looked like the models who wore their clothes, but how would I know? Remember, I had never met them.

Of course, in the end I did drag myself to the opening. Luckily, by the time I got there, the store was so jam-packed with people that no one even noticed me. It was every inch the "happening" that Paul had said it would be. He hired Andy Warhol to produce the event, and Warhol in turn got The Velvet Underground to perform. He also got Pattie Boyd, Marisa Berenson, and Jean Shrimpton to walk around the party modeling clothes while go-go dancers shimmied in the store windows amusing the large crowd out on the sidewalk trying to get in.

The whole thing was loud, loud, loud! All of the other designers were proudly showing off and talking about their clothes to anyone who would listen while I skulked around anonymously, feeling out of place. I had practically nothing there to show off. I had nothing to do. I stayed for about a half hour before sneaking out, getting on the subway, and going home, where I had a nice long cry.

The next morning I was up early and at the studio at eight o'clock, just as I had been every other day before the opening. I was ready to put that depressing evening behind me and just keep going.

My clothes were delivered a couple of days later, and I finally was able to see my things in a store setting. I almost cried again, I was so proud of how everything looked, *especially* the label. However, when I went back to the store a few days later I was concerned: most of my stuff was gone. The racks were practically empty. Hysterically I asked the salesgirls what had happened to my clothes. They looked at me like I was crazy and said, "Well, they were *sold*, of course." I didn't know what to say. I mean, obviously, I was elated. To think girls whom I didn't even know were running around town in my stuff!

Paul even called me that night to congratulate me on my "sell-through," which I learned was retailese for "my stuff sold." The production people also called, asking when they could get more samples. All of a sudden it was like, *Okay, time to get serious.* We never followed what I now know is a proper design

Twiggy in Betsey!

Anouk Aimée in my long-john nightshirt dress made of silvery jersey

In my messy workroom

schedule. In the real world you design and produce so many collections per season. There are two seasons per year—fall and spring. At Paraphernalia we designed stuff constantly. If it was summer we produced summer clothes; in winter we produced winter clothes and so on . . .

I didn't actually go to Paraphernalia very often, but I remember Paul coming into the store one time I did happen to be there. It was a cold December day, and he went off the rails when he saw that there were no coats in the store. So you guessed it. I rushed back to the studio and designed a bunch of coats. Tulah and I worked on the patterns that night, and the samples were ready in a couple of days. Paul had coats in the store just in time for the first blizzard of the season. This experience taught me another retail term, "wear-now." The people who shopped at Paraphernalia were definitely not the types who planned ahead. There was a popular saying at the time: you go to Paraphernalia for clothes to *wear* out on Saturday night and *throw* out on Sunday morning. We were definitely a wear-now store.

Rock bands, artists, hip downtown kids and their uptown wannabe counterparts came to shop at Paraphernalia or just hang out. It was the only place to get the far-out kinds of clothes they wanted to wear. *And* it was unisex! Which was a totally unique concept for the time. With the exception of department stores, men and women had previously shopped at completely separate places.

This was a dream job for me if ever there was one. And it

With Michael Mott, Paul Young, and some models wearing our designs

*Penelope Tree in the outfit I designed for her to wear to
Truman Capote's Black and White Ball in 1966*

Veruschka in my Enkalure nylon bathing suit

wasn't just a one-way street. Paraphernalia was very good for me, but I was also very good for Paraphernalia. I consistently outsold all of the other designers in the store. I may not have made the most money for the company, because right from the get-go I designed with one eye on creativity and the other on affordability. I told Paul that I didn't want any of my clothing to cost more than ninety-nine dollars, which I equated to the cost of a weekend in Puerto Rico. That was the yardstick I used; very scientific.

And believe me, as hard as I was working I also took many ninety-nine-dollar weekends in Puerto Rico!

5.) I MARRIED THE VELVET UNDERGROUND (WELL, NOT ALL OF THEM)

I have always said that of all my three and a half husbands (I'll explain that later), John Cale was by far my favorite.

Paraphernalia became a particular favorite hangout of The Velvet Underground after they played at the opening night party. I had already met the band some time earlier at Max's Kansas City and had recently started going out with their lead guitarist, Sterling Morrison. It was nothing serious, just a few dates here and there.

Sometime around 1965, when Paraphernalia really began to take off, was when I made the leap from just hanging out with the band to actually making clothes for all the Velvets: Sterling, Maureen Tucker, John Cale, and Lou Reed, but, oddly enough, not Nico. I tried to get her to wear my designs, but she really liked creating her own. She didn't make those famous white suits she wore, but she did come up with some very bohemian caftan-y things, like the one she wears on the cover of her *Desertshore* album. As for Lou, all *he* ever wanted was a motorcycle jacket and gray suede trousers. His only suggestion was to cut the pants very, very tight through the crotch. He always said that I cut a good crotch.

While I did love the Velvets' music, I was just as intrigued by their whole scene, and the crazy ways that everyone lived—up all night, sleeping all day. And party after party after party dressed in one fabulous, far-out look after another. The plastic dresses, the paper dresses, the *electric* dresses! Everything was so new. And didn't anybody work?! It was the complete opposite of my world. At the Velvets' shows, inhibitions went right out the window, and people went crazy . . . literally. John read me a review in *Variety* that called one of their appearances "a three-ring psychosis." To me that sounded very scary. As much as I was energized by the insanity, I was not at all tempted to dive in.

The Velvets' show I remember best was at the Dom on St. Marks Place in April 1966. Andy Warhol produced the event, which he called "Andy Warhol Presents—The Exploding Plastic Inevitable." I had no idea what to expect, but given that Andy had creative control, I figured I'd better be wearing an amazing outfit. Since I was going to the show straight from Paraphernalia, I grabbed one of my Silverfish dresses. That's the same one that Edie would be photographed in the night of the Chelsea

Hotel fire a few months later and Karen Black would totally rock in *Easy Rider.* I wore the dress with a new pair of silver stack-heeled Mary Janes and pale lipstick. I was ready to sparkle.

What a trip! I walked into the Dom and plunged into darkness. Andy's movies were being projected on the walls, the ceiling, and even the crowd, so I was walking through *My Hustler* and *Poor Little Rich Girl* as I tried to make my way closer to the stage. When Nico and the band started in with "Femme Fatale" at a deafening volume, the most amazing light show started. Crazy, bright-colored strobes gave me strange, quick bursts of

The Velvet Underground providing the appropriate electric soundtrack for the Paraphernalia opening

The Dom on St. Marks Place. <u>Not</u> my thing.

images from the nearly black room. It was like being stuck in a huge kaleidoscope.

The strobe lights broke down every moment of the Velvets' performance into dazzling fractions of a second. Lou or Nico or John would be singled out, mixed in with random faces and bodies in the crowd. I could catch a glimpse now and then of Gerard Malanga and Mary Woronov doing their infamous whip dance—living out their S & M fantasies right onstage. Edie Sedgwick, oblivious to the whip, go-go danced alongside them. With the volume of "All Tomorrow's Parties" rattling me to the core, I could see flashes in the audience of clothing I

Edie in my "Snap-Apart" outfit

had designed and sold just days earlier. My heart was pounding. I almost felt seasick. I wasn't doing any drugs, but being so disoriented was starting to take a toll on me. Only recently had I started to think of myself as a jaded New Yorker, but as the lights hit another crazy reflector, I started to feel like that small-town girl I didn't want to lose. I may have been surrounded by ecstatic friends and customers, but some vague notion of designing for a spunky girl who wouldn't get sucked into *the plastic inevitable* helped send me to the door.

Outside the chilly April air felt great. Walking back to my

loft on LaGuardia Place, my ears still ringing, I couldn't even begin to process everything I'd seen. But that was okay. I knew I'd be up for work before nine a.m. and perhaps design another version of my stretch silver T-shirt dress that would move on Edie like an alien skin and look great under strobe lights.

As for my own wants and needs, I started thinking more about John Cale and less about Sterling. Even if I did leave the Velvets' shows early, I was becoming more and more attracted to John's musical genius. He was classically trained but played the edgiest rock keyboards, bass, and viola. John was tall and thin with long dark hair and dark eyes to match. He was quiet—brooding, even—and he was Welsh. He actually grew up speaking *only* Welsh, and I was just a sucker for that accent. I loved it when he spoke to me in his native tongue. It's such a brutal-sounding language. When he talked to me that way, I never needed to know *what* he was saying.

Well, one thing led to another, and Sterling was out, and John was in. I mean, we just clicked. He could make me laugh like no one else, which has always been superimportant to me in a relationship. If you can't make me laugh, it ain't gonna happen.

I also loved the way John's brain worked. He had a hyperactive mind that seemed to know something intriguing about almost everything. After a long day of churning out as many new fashion ideas as possible for Paraphernalia, I found listening to John endlessly amusing. He did sometimes lose me when he went off on one of his conspiracy theories. Remember, this was just a couple of years after the Kennedy assassination, and John had a thousand theories about what had "really" happened. He was more about finding a good story, I think, than delivering any hard-and-fast truth.

Since John was a poet, after all, I designed clothes for him to look the part. There's something very intimate about making a garment for someone you're really into. I made him these great black canvas suits that were perfect for his build and some fancy shirts with ruffles. They were gorgeous and fit perfectly with my fantasy of John.

We weren't dating for long before we knew we were crazy mad about each other. John told me that he liked me because I was a happy person and I made him feel comfortable, which I took as pretty high praise. I think he was looking for me to be a stabilizing factor in his life, which was pretty chaotic. He didn't want me to be a drug buddy or Warhol fabulous. In a way we were both dreaming much more Norman Rockwell. Almost immediately he moved in with me.

At the time, I was living in a huge loft on LaGuardia Place just a block or so north of Houston Street. This was before Soho was even a thing. There was no reason to go there. It was just a bunch of warehouses. The loft was huge, over three thousand square feet. It was more than big enough for me to have my workshop there and for John to store all of his instruments and use the space as his home office and meeting place. It was basically just a big empty space with the walls and ceiling painted white and the floor painted gray, very raw.

The space was so big that we really only lived in a corner of it, where I built us a kind of dollhouse of a room. It was just tall enough for John to stand up in comfortably. It had a loft bed and lots of space for storing clothes. I may have seen a fairy-tale castle when I squinted at our room, but it was more like a glorified walk-in closet with a door and two windows.

Nico used to visit us pretty often as she and John were really close. In fact, they were roommates right before he moved in. When she'd come over she loved to crouch down in the crawl space beneath the huge industrial sink in the kitchen, relax, and sew her own clothes for hours. Nico had always had a reputation for being cold, but I liked her. I found her to be very sweet. I think the "cold" reputation had more to do with her shyness, being German, and, of course, the language barrier. Her English wasn't very good, but she had an interesting way of speaking and it added a very distinctive style to her singing. Very Dietrich, very Garbo.

John and I hadn't been together all that long when one day out of the blue, out of nowhere, I can't even remember whose idea it was, we decided to get married. But that was typical of the times. Back then everything just seemed to happen in a flash. The pace was quicker, and there was a real feeling of urgency. Everything was now, now, now and about grabbing life and running with it. So we figured, why not? We ran with it.

Just the love—John's and my wedding-photo shoot

When I was growing up, I'd always dreamt I would have the fancy church wedding with all the bridesmaids and flowers and of course the big Cinderella dress. But somehow I got talked into tying the knot at drab, dreary City Hall.

In the late sixties the unisex trend was very big, so for the occasion, instead of a ballgown, I made myself a beautiful burgundy crushed velvet Edwardian-style pantsuit and a white silk blouse with a bow at the neck. I was so proud of that outfit. I also made John a matching suit in black.

Besides making the clothes, all we really needed to do before the wedding was get a blood test. Since neither of us had a regular doctor, we were happy for a referral to the offices of doctors Bishop and Jacobson. After one of the kind doctors took our blood he gave us a shot of "vitamins." I don't know what was in those shots, but by the time we left the office we were out of our minds. We walked all the way downtown from Eighty-Sixth Street, babbling the whole way about how fabulous our marriage was going to be. I found out later that these two physicians were notorious "speed doctors" to the stars. Sitting in the waiting room I should have known something wasn't right when I saw large canisters filled with pills and people helping themselves by the handful, like they were candy.

But we did get our blood tests, and our wedding day was a week later. John and I got dressed with a whole crowd of friends at the loft. It was quite a group gathered to wish us well: Andy, Nico, Lou, Sterling, Maureen, Viva, Billy Name, Ondine, and a few random models.

Oddly enough my mother and father weren't there. That's a good indication of how seriously I took the wedding or how slapdash the whole thing came together. It never occurred to me to invite my family. My parents had met John only a couple of times. I brought him to Connecticut not long after we got together. They didn't *dislike* him. How could they? They were actually charmed by him, especially my mother. But they just didn't know what to make of this longhaired guy wearing

Beatle boots and all-black clothing. He certainly didn't look like the man they had envisioned me marrying. He was from a whole other planet than Leo Macawicz.

When we were dressed and ready for City Hall, we all jumped into taxis and arrived en masse. We were quite the spectacle, and for once it wasn't about the way people were dressed, as there were no sequins or feather boas. Instead it was the group energy—quirky, kinetic, and loud!

I had butterflies in my stomach—or it could have been the diet pills I had started taking that were making me nervous—but other than that I was happy and excited as we walked inside. Then I realized that John hadn't thought to bring me flowers, and I just began to cry. Me, of all people, without flowers on my wedding day. Luckily someone had the presence of mind to run out and buy me gardenias from one of the flower vendors who hung around outside City Hall for just that purpose. That helped calm me down.

So there we were, speedily chattering away in a waiting room with a whole bunch of normal people also hoping to see the judge and get married as quickly as possible. Andy was milling around tape recording conversations with some of the other couples and snapping Polaroids. He'd just walk up to them and say something like "Wow! You look fabulous!" They had no idea who he was, even though he was then the most famous artist in New York City.

At last our names were called, and we stood in front of the

judge, who was a very stern, serious-looking old man. He scanned our group with a disapproving glance, finally settling his gaze on me, and said in his deep, judgmental voice, "Young lady, I will not marry a girl who is wearing pants!" Can you imagine?

What was I supposed to do? I was heartbroken and more than that, really angry. Of all the things for someone to say on my special day, and a judge no less. But I didn't realize that this was the norm. I had a real downtown mentality and had no idea that my wearing a pantsuit might be questionable to someone like him. Remember, in 1967 most women still dressed with a 1950s mind-set and wouldn't go out without their gloves matching their purses.

Then I had an idea. I told John to wait a minute and went to the ladies' room, where I removed my offending pants, readjusted my tights, pulled my jacket down as far as it would go (which wasn't very far), examined myself in the mirror, and defiantly walked back out. I took my place next to John (whose jaw, along with everybody else's, was on the floor) and said all proper, "Okay, your honor, I am *not* wearing pants. Will you marry us now?" And he did.

After that we all went over to Ratner's deli and had a huge breakfast. It was a very fitting start for what was to be a rather unconventional marriage.

There was no time for a honeymoon after our wedding day. I had deadlines to meet for Paraphernalia, and John was in rehearsals to go on tour with the band. Strange that we didn't even think about a honeymoon, because we both loved to travel. Just a few weeks earlier we had gone to Wales to visit John's parents.

They lived in a small town called Garnant. It was very industrial and, well, to call it bleak would be a compliment. The landscape was what I would describe as gothic. It was filled with large twisted trees, like the set of an old black-and-white horror movie. And it was *cold*. There was no heat in the house, and we had to bring a hot water bottle to bed with us to keep from freezing.

John's mom was a schoolteacher, and his father was a coal miner, which is what all the men in town seemed to do for a living. His hands were permanently stained black. I knew it was a hard life, but I didn't know what to make of his parents sitting down at night to watch Tom and Jerry cartoons on television. John assured me that his mother was crazy about me, although I wouldn't have known because she spoke only Welsh—and coming from her, it was hardly the romance language it was coming from John.

We stayed about a week, and it was interesting to see John on his home turf, although he hadn't lived there since he was about seventeen. He didn't seem very close with his parents— not like the way I was with mine—and especially not with his father, who would rather pick up a newspaper than have a conversation. We spent a lot of time alone walking through the countryside, which I found isolating and depressing compared to my storybook memories of my home in Connecticut.

But the trip was romantic in its own *Wuthering Heights* kind of way. I felt I got more insight into John and his music. I recall thinking, *My God, if this surreal landscape is his home, it's no wonder his music is so out there!*

For someone who was becoming a real city girl, I still had those small-town values deeply instilled in me and had it in my head that John and I were going to have a "normal" marriage. I wanted to make pot roast every Sunday night just like my mom did. Even John said that he wanted a real "pipe and slippers" kind of home life. Well, *that* lasted about two weeks. We could *not* stick to a regular routine. I was a day person, and John was a real night owl. A rock musician doesn't keep regular hours and show up at home just because I happen to make a roast. Not that I was immune myself to staying up all night occasionally to meet deadlines.

I was aware when I met John that he was taking drugs. That was no surprise and certainly not unusual. In that period absolutely everyone was on something, except me, if you don't count the diet pills. It was a huge, huge part of the culture. But that druggy aspect of the whole scene actually scared me. So many people would be around for a while and then one day they'd suddenly be gone. If you asked what had happened to them, the answer was always the same: either they'd OD'd, or they were put away in an institution, or in some cases both. And that scared the hell out of me.

While I *was* frightened by John's drug use, I'd be lying if I said that I didn't also find it intriguing, and even sexy. Before meeting John and his crowd, I didn't know people who did drugs. And maybe I was making excuses for him but I viewed it through a twisted lens and in my mind dubbed him a tortured artist.

As for my own "weight-loss medications," I convinced myself that was different. After all, they were prescribed by a doctor. It wasn't like I bought them in a back alley. I had to go way, way out on the subway to somewhere in Queens to get the drugs. It was a really sketchy set-up. Now that I think back, I'm sure the guy dispensing the stuff wasn't a doctor at all. Sometimes it was pills, and other times he'd give me this liquid that I had to take two drops of in the morning and two drops in the afternoon. The truth is, I was buzzing around day and night just as much as everyone on the scene who was shooting amphetamines, so who was I to judge?

John was never really open with me about the drugs, but I would sometimes find a needle in our bathroom, or see him conspiring in a corner backstage before one of the Velvets' shows. It wasn't long before I realized he was practically living the lyrics to Lou's song "Heroin," with its line that goes "Heroin, it's my life and it's my wife." That seemed to sum up our relationship perfectly around our third month of marriage. I guess I assumed it was his business, I knew what I was getting into when we met, so there was really nothing I could say. I started going to work every day wondering if he'd be alive when I got home and the stress of all that uncertainty began to take its toll on me.

I know John originally wanted to marry me because, in his words, I was a "nice" girl. And apparently there was a shortage of nice girls around. But nice is no reason to get married and nice can get a relationship only so far. I did try to interject normalcy when I could, but after a while he just wasn't receptive. By the time of our first anniversary, John and I hardly talked and the sex that had been a huge part of our relationship at the beginning was nonexistent. I threw myself into my work and tried to ignore what had become of my marriage because I had no idea how to fix it.

Our marriage problems weren't confined to our home life. They spilled over into John's professional life as well. I knew that Lou Reed thought that I had come between him and John. I've joked in the past that I was the Yoko Ono of The Velvet Underground even though I wasn't trying to steal John away from anyone. But Lou had always been a little bit in love with John and hated it when John's attentions were not 100 percent on the band. I always felt uncomfortable with the negative vibe I got from Lou. It's no secret that there was never any love lost between the two of us after John and I got together. Lou never directly confronted me, and we had no arguments, but there might be a sneer or a dirty look from him when I walked into the room or a dismissive reference to me as "that girl who makes the clothes." And that hurt. I worked too hard to be referred to that way.

Not long after John and I were married Lou called a band

meeting without inviting John and told Maureen and Sterling that either John went or he would. I think we all know which way that wind ended up blowing. John was out. Lou called it creative differences. They each had their own ideas about the future direction of the band. This much was definitely true: Lou wanted commercial success, and the stuff John wanted to do was not often radio friendly, which was key back then to hitting it big.

I think Lou was envious of John's musical virtuosity as well. At the end of the day, Lou owed a great deal to John, who brought a very distinctive sound to the band. You can hear it if you listen to some of John's early work, for example, "The Theater of Eternal Music." There's a specific drone that he got from the modified viola that he played. You can hear the same sound in songs like "Venus in Furs" and also the piano part that he played on "All Tomorrow's Parties." Without John, the Velvets would have been just a straightforward rock band. A *good* rock band, mind you. Lou was a great musician and an amazing lyricist. A line like "Different colors made of tears"? That's brilliant. But without John, the Velvets wouldn't have had that experimental avant-garde sound that set them apart from all the other bands.

John, of course, was devastated that the Velvets had kicked him out, and because we weren't communicating with each other very much, I didn't know how to make it better. John decided that he needed to go to California to try to get clean and figure out what to do next. I thought to myself, *Well, that doesn't make* any *sense. They have drugs out there, too.*

We both knew I couldn't go with him—not that I was even invited. My work was in New York, and I wouldn't leave it for him. He had to go and do this on his own. After John left we'd talk on the phone, but in those days three thousand miles seemed a lot farther away than it does today. It wasn't long before the calls became fewer and farther between.

I don't know who made the decision to finalize the split. It seemed obvious to both of us. There was no blame game. When it came time to sign the divorce papers, I got on a plane and brought them out to California myself. At that point John was living with another woman, and I was seeing someone, too. I

John shortly after our divorce

told myself I could handle it. I was even planning to stay with John and Cindy, who would soon become his next wife.

When I arrived I tried to be upbeat and in control, but it didn't work. Cindy knew enough not to be around, and that night John and I hung out alone in his living room. He lit candles, we drank wine, and he ended up playing piano for me. It was a very tender gesture and almost more than I could bear. *This* was the John I had fallen in love with. This is who John *really* is. But I was crushed. He was still on drugs, and I couldn't deal with the fact that he was with someone else (even though I was, too). We signed the papers, and I left the next day.

My mother's way of acknowledging the breakup was to send me a box of chocolate chip cookies that she had baked herself. I'm sure I could not bear to eat them.

After all these years I've remained close with John. We went years without speaking, but our paths eventually began to cross. I would see him in New York at some event or other and I've always loved and followed his music. This past year I went with him to the Grammys, where he received his lifetime achievement award for his work with the Velvets. The press credited me as "The Velvet Underground fashion designer," and I couldn't be prouder of that title or of the relationship I have with John now. Like I said earlier, he was my favorite husband.

6.) "HAVE A NICE DAY!" ALLEY CAT.

I decided to leave Paraphernalia when it started to fizzle. By 1969 they had overexpanded when they went the franchise route. All of a sudden, *anyone* who had ten thousand dollars to spare could open a Paraphernalia store. With these stores, more often than not, the formula got watered down, and the stores didn't seem special anymore. Paraphernalia also expanded into concept shops in a few department stores in Philly and DC, and they failed miserably. The clothes in these shops were so crazy looking that people wouldn't set foot inside. The powers that be thought that the general public was ready for our designs but the*y were not*. They overlooked the fact that what made Paraphernalia special was that the store was unique *and* it was in New York City. Not the best yardstick by which to measure the rest of the country . . . not by a long shot.

I think the real reason Paraphernalia was going down the tubes was that it just wasn't relevant anymore. By the late sixties it was passé, even in New York. The store had been such a huge part of the sixties, and I think that's the point: the sixties were *over*. They'd OD'd. Janice Joplin was dead. Jimi Hendrix was dead. When we finally *did* make it to the moon, we found out there was nothing there.

I wasn't the only one who was dissatisfied/disillusioned with Paraphernalia; so were two of my coworkers, Barbara Washburn, whom we called Bunky, and Anita Latorre, whom we called Nini. We all agreed that the reason Paraphernalia existed in the first place just didn't apply anymore. We talked about opening our own store. One that would embrace the original concept: a true designer collective that felt special. Bunky would be in charge of the business end of things. Nini would be the buyer and merchandiser. My part of the equation would be to do my own line of funky, real handsy-crafty things. It was a nice idea, and at that point just a fantasy. Something to take our minds off our work situation.

Even though I had made up my mind to leave, I didn't do anything as foolish as quit right away. I planned to go to Paul and ask him for a substantial raise, to basically double my salary. If he went for it, great, I'd stay and tough it out, but I knew he wouldn't. You have to be fully prepared to walk when you put yourself in a situation like that and I was *more* than ready.

I called Paul at his office and was surprised that he was in. I thought I'd be leaving a message with the receptionist. I didn't want to have this conversation over the phone. As much as I hated confrontation of any kind I liked and respected Paul and wanted to be upfront with him and I preferred to speak with him face-to-face.

I asked him if I could come over to see him, that I had something important to talk to him about. He said, "You're leaving Paraphernalia, aren't you?" I was shocked. I thought I had a pretty good poker face and had no idea he could tell I wasn't happy there anymore. I stammered and asked, "How did you know?" "I'm a pretty sharp guy," he replied and made the conversation very easy. He told me that he would be sorry to see me go and that he always loved working with me and never once regretted hiring me. He was incredibly gracious about it and was interested in what I was planning to do.

I gave him as sketchy a version of my plans as I could. Bunky and Nini were still working there, and I didn't want to screw up their situation. I knew they were both planning to quit any day now as well.

At the end of the call, Paul wished me well and told me if I ever needed anything, I should not hesitate to call him.

It went much better than I could have hoped. And I was

glad for it. One very important rule to learn in life is that you never, ever leave on bad terms, not if you can help it. You never burn a bridge. No matter what industry you work in, I can guarantee that it's a small world, and you'll end up running into the same people over and over.

A couple of days later, after tying up loose ends, it was time for me to clear out my Paraphernalia workspace and move on. This was easy. For me, once something is over, it's over. I don't get all nostalgic and misty eyed. I simply took down the sketches that completely covered all the walls of my workroom, packed up boxes of what I'd need to take with me, and left what I didn't. I think it took me all of an hour to put that phase of my life behind me.

Opening a store with Bunky and Nini was just one of the plots rattling around in my brain. I also entertained the thought of designing for an established label. I even went as far as to put some feelers out to Young Arpreggio, Crazy Horse, and a few of the other junior labels that interested me. I had been operating in a bubble at Paraphernalia for more than four years and I had no idea what the current climate was in the fashion industry. Boy, was I about to find out!

Instead of being respected for the designing I had done at Paraphernalia, I found that I had acquired an undeserved reputation. Practically everyone I spoke to believed that anyone associated with Paraphernalia was into the whole drug scene. After how hard I had worked, that assumption wasn't fair. I was crushed.

Just as I had expected, Bunky and Nini ended up quitting just a few days after I spoke with Paul.

Given my undeserved reputation, I was so thankful that they still wanted to do the store thing. Not only did they want to open a store, but before I even knew what was happening, Bunky found a location—an old brownstone on Fifty-Third Street between Second and Third avenues. This little strip not far from Bloomingdale's was just starting to become a retail hotspot. Kind of like a little Carnaby Street with specialty boutiques and the famous ice cream shop Serendipity Three.

We were on the the ground floor of the building, which had been an apartment, so it was set up as a series of rooms. One of them would be the Betsey room and feature only my designs. I papered its walls with a beautiful floral pattern, and then moved in all of my merchandise. After a buying trip to Europe, Bunky and Nini soon had the other rooms filled with great designer duds as well. Next we hired some hip girls we knew from the other downtown scene to work in the store. In fact, one of the girls we hired was Kim Hastreiter, who went on to become co-founder of *Paper* magazine.

Within a couple of months of leaving Paraphernalia we were running our own shop. I was busy at night making my samples, which I had copied in sewing rooms in Chinatown, some of the same ones that had made my Paraphernalia clothing. I was designing things that were the complete opposite of the stuff I was doing at Paraphernalia. I was getting back to my

Nini Latorre, Bunky Washburn, and me in the Betsey Bunky Nini store

Me with models in Little Italy—Fall/Winter 1972 Ready-to-Wear Collection

With models in the Garment District—Fall/Winter 1972
Ready-to-Wear Collection

country-girl roots, doing prairie dresses and using lots of cal-
ico. I was also revisiting my obsession with petticoats, but with
a cowgirl vibe.

Right off the bat the store did very well, and we became a
destination for the hip uptown girls that didn't want to go
downtown. It didn't take me long to realize that being a partner at Betsey Bunky Nini wouldn't make me enough money to
live on. I needed to find a full-time gig, so I started to seriously
look for a job this time and not just test the waters.

But I soon found out that not only would nobody hire
me, I couldn't even get people to return my phone calls. My

supposed reputation aside, it turned out I also lacked the proper degree to get any kind of design position. Remember, at school I majored in art, not fashion, and these "real" companies wanted the right kind of credentials. It was ridiculous and so unfair. I had already made a real name for myself designing for Paraphernalia and assumed *that* would have given me at least *some* street cred. But it didn't. People insisted that I have the proper training.

I was really in a funk. It wasn't just my professional life that was frustrating, but my personal life was, too. My recent divorce had me depressed and licking my wounds. I felt as if I just wanted to go away somewhere to a cabin in the woods and sit by a fire and be comfortable. You know, that whole seventies *Have a nice day* vibe.

People had started using that expression a lot. It was a hippie-dippie thing, and one I never really liked. It sounded forced and fake to me. I thought people were using the phrase ironically, because there were actually a lot of dark things going on in the world, politically speaking. Not that I ever got remotely involved in politics. I've never found any of that stuff very interesting. That said, it was pretty hard, even for me, who much preferred to live in the fantasy world going on in my head, to ignore all of the protest marches that were taking place across the country.

While there may have been political storm clouds swirling overhead, I must have still had at least one lucky star up there as well. I'll explain.

Nini had a boyfriend named Les, who happened to be playing basketball one day at the Y with a friend of his named Norman. They were talking as they played, like you do, and Les told Norman how unhappy Nini and the rest of us had been at Paraphernalia and that we had started this new gig. My name came up, and Norman, who happened to be the sales director for a clothing company called Alley Cat, of course knew about Paraphernalia and had heard of me. He told Les that his company was looking for a new designer and asked if it was okay to give me a call.

Norman phoned me the very next day, and after a brief conversation we scheduled an appointment. A few days later I went to see him at his office at 1407 Broadway in the Garment District, which was coincidentally right down the block from where I had first met Paul Young. This time around I didn't drag two bulging suitcases of designs to show. The only thing I brought was my reputation. Les had told me that Norman was actually a fan of my work with Paraphernalia.

For the meeting I wore some of the new stuff I was making. By this point I, along with most of the women of America, had ditched their miniskirts, which now looked tacky and outdated. Like Isaac Newton said, "What goes up, must come down." This was bad news for my mother. She had only recently taken to wearing shorter skirts! I had begun making and wearing midi skirts, which hit right about mid shin. This new length looked and felt fresh. When I arrived at 1407, I marched right up to Norman's office and I liked him right away. Where Paul was a quirky, artistic, visionary type, Norman was the complete opposite. He was a big bear of a guy and a total garmento. He didn't sell *fashion*, he sold *clothing*.

As we sat down in his *very* lived-in office, he explained that with the Alley Cat label, they were trying to capture the junior market, which they felt was almost completely untapped and had huge potential *if* they could find the right designer. They had already tried out a few people but couldn't find anyone who made the cut. The most recent designers who didn't make the cut were Willi Smith and Carol Horn. Both were very talented, and I admired their work, so I was feeling a little bit intimidated but I didn't let that get to me because right from the start I had a good feeling about the company.

Norman went on to tell me his boss was a man named Leonard Shandal who operated the business out of his office in North Philadelphia. Leonard owned Alley Cat and a couple of other labels. His current focus was one called Le d'Amour, which made women's plus-size clothes.

The wheels in my brain were spinning, and I thought that this could be a great set-up for me. Alley Cat was in New York City, and Leonard had his own deal in North Philly, which in my feverish brain meant the big boss man would be far enough away to leave me alone to do my work. Another thing that appealed to me about this potential new gig was the huge volume of clothing that Alley Cat produced. At Paraphernalia I always felt a bit stifled by the small quantities we ran. I was into mass production in a major way because I knew you couldn't make an affordable garment unless you made it in large quantities. The more you make of something, the cheaper it can be. Not to mention that I wanted to see *everyone* in my clothes.

My designs while at Paraphernalia were too much for the masses, too crazy. Middle America would never have gone for them. But by the early seventies I had caught up with the masses—or they had caught up with me. I'm not sure which, but I felt as if the masses were more like me now. I had a genuinely optimistic attitude, and I truly believed that I wasn't *that* weird. If *I* liked something, then there had to be lots of other girls who would like it, too.

I told Norman that I was definitely interested in the position but I had some conditions I needed to discuss with him before giving him my answer. I had some great press from Paraphernalia, which earlier in our conversation he told me he had seen, so I knew I could put my tiny foot down and exercise a certain amount of control over the job. My heart told me that if I didn't have control, it wouldn't work out.

First of all, I wanted the freedom to design what I wanted and to be left alone to do it. If he could deliver on that one, I promised I could make it happen. I don't know where this confidence came from. But there it was.

Second, I wanted my name on the label. I still didn't realize what a luxury that was.

Third, I explained my involvement with Betsey Bunky Nini

and told him that I wanted the freedom to use the workroom to continue making those clothes as well, explaining that this was a prior commitment I still needed to honor, assuring him I was capable of doing both.

Fourth, I wanted to decorate the wholesale showroom myself and asked for two weeks to do it.

Lastly, I wanted to hire the girls who would work in the showroom selling the line to the wholesale market, and I wanted to train them myself. I knew I'd need girls who would understand the clothes, and it was very important that the girls *got* me.

Out of breath I finished my tempest-in-a-teapot performance. Good-natured Norman, with his arms folded over his big barrel chest, was smiling and said he'd have to think about it. That broad smile told me that he wouldn't need much time. I left the meeting feeling about ten pounds lighter than when I went in and floated home, fantasizing about leaving the dated silver slickness of the previous decade behind me.

The next morning, bright and early, Norman called to tell me that I had the job if I wanted it and that he was happy to comply with my "demands." He ended the conversation by observing that I was certainly a gal who knew what she wanted, and that he liked that quality in a person. It made his job easier.

I was so eager to start right away and Norman was even more eager, as I was now going to be on the fashion calendar, which had specific seasons, delivery dates, and regularly scheduled fashion shows. At Paraphernalia we were never on any calendar other than Paul's. I was going to need to get a move on.

Before I sat down to design a single piece of clothing, my first plan of action at Alley Cat was to decorate the two show-rooms. As much as I wanted the showrooms to reflect my personality, it was also important to me that buyers *get* what I was doing with my clothing designs. The decorating helped set the mood for the clothes they'd be looking at. I had definite ideas as to what I wanted the sales rooms to look like. At Paraphernalia it was *their* world—all that chrome, Lucite, and mirrored surfaces—and that just wasn't me anymore. I'm not sure if it ever was. I wanted to go back to Connecticut, back to the country, and back to dancing school.

In the first room I painted murals on all the walls, ceiling, and even parts of the floor: a complete environment, total immersion. I started at the baseboards painting grass on them and in the grass I painted worms and little bugs. Then I worked my way up the walls into flowers and trees and onto a bright blue sky with fluffy clouds and colorful birds. In the background a big cloud-covered mountain loomed over my fantasy landscape. It was all very organic but painted in the most intense colors. It was like one of the sets from my childhood recitals.

The other room had a completely different feel. I covered the walls with vintage wallpaper (similar to what I had done at

Betsey Bunky Nini), which I found at Secondhand Rose's in Tribeca. It was printed with huge bunches of white flowers on a blue-gray background, very English country garden.

It was a lot of work, and when I finally finished I realized that I had practically lived in those two rooms twenty-four hours a day for two weeks.

My next task was to hire a couple of salesgirls. Norman ran an ad in *Women's Wear Daily*, and I interviewed the applicants to make sure they were just right.

Only then did I get down to work. Leonard, true to his word and ninety miles away in Philadelphia, left me alone and I started to design. My gig at Alley Cat marked the beginning of my obsessive collecting. I began to surround myself with familiar objects that I liked to look at and draw. I would sketch everything I saw if it struck a chord. If I was sitting on a cutesy chair I would draw it. If I bought an Art Deco teapot at the Chelsea flea market, I'd sketch that, or dolls, or flowers, and on and on. I turned into a real human sketching machine. In doing so I was developing a whole new work process. The objects I was sketching played into the little storybook life that was always going on in my head and would eventually end up in my designs. For example, the Deco teapot became a motif on an unusual quilted maxi coat.

I was interested in doing knits, so the first things I worked on were jacquard sweaters. I'd start by doing an obsessively detailed drawing. When I was finished with it, I'd work with a

Exterior view of the Paraphernalia store, designed by Ulrich Franzen, who went on to design Hunter College and Cooper Union in the ugly brutalist style that became *huge* in the 1970s.

Two *Very* Different Examples of My Work at Paraphernalia

Donuts, diamonds, and zigzags: Early minidresses actually just skimmed the knees, as skirts didn't get *really* short until a few years later.

My clothes started to creep into other areas of the design world, such as in this ad featuring the Silverfish top and foil miniskirt for Eero Saarinen for Knoll.

Julie Christie wearing my Julie Christie in *Mademoiselle* magazine.

Edie Sedgwick in Silverfish (with bandaged hands as a result of the Chelsea Hotel fire she had started).

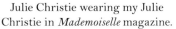

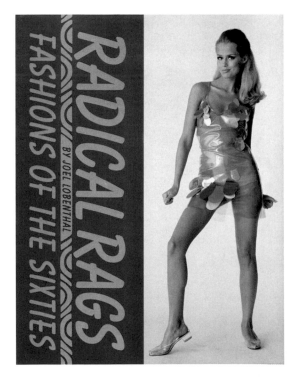

Cover girl Lauren Hutton in my "Kit" dress. This clear dress came in a box along with colored shapes that could be applied wherever you wanted, based on how naughty or nice you were feeling.

Some of the styles I
did for Butterick Patterns.

Butterick **6531**
THE FASHION ONE $1.00

SIZE 10
BUST 32½

YOUNG DESIGNER
Betsey
Johnson
of Alley Cat

JUNIOR
5 7 9 11 13

MISSES'
6 8 10 12

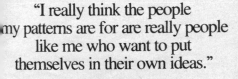

"I really think the people
my patterns are for are really people
like me who want to put
themselves in their own ideas."

When I was at Alley Cat, I was
approached by the people at Butterick
Patterns. It turned out that people loved
to make my clothes in fabrics they chose
themselves. I have no explanation for
my hairstyle at the time!

Peruvian People prints.
One of my very first complicated knits.

Patchwork
corduroy jacket
with faux monkey
fur sleeves. I was
inspired by those
fabulous 1930s
designs by Adrian
in movies like
The Women, which
I love!

Floral-printed quilted corduroy maxicoat. This was featured in a huge spread for *Seventeen* magazine, the title of which was "Betsey Johnson shows you how to get it all together."

Another outfit from the *Seventeen* spread. When they called me about this project, they told me I could do whatever I wanted to do . . . and I did!

"Wizard of Oz" coat with diamond underwear underneath (not shown in photograph).

More complicated sweater designs. These are the ones that made the graphics guy's head spin. He was the guy who was responsible for transforming my incredibly detailed designs into something that would work on the knitting machines.

BELTED BUTTERFLIES FOR BOTH. JAVIER IN HIS/HERS TURTLE SWEATER TOP. #9602 $66.00 MAGENTA OR BLUE GROUND (SEE PAGE 10). ONE SIZE. MATCHING LEGGINGS #9610 $56.00. ONE SIZE. XIMENIA SHOWS OFF HER CREW NECK SHOULDER-PADDED STRAIGHT CUT SWEATER DRESS #9603 $78.00. MAGENTA OR BLUE. ONE SIZE. BLACK PATENT 2" WIDE WAIST/HIP BELT #2"-B $20.00. 3" WIDE BLACK PATENT WRIST/ANKLE BELT #3" WAB $12.00.

5

My 1980s return to printed knits. As well as butterflies, I did pterodactyls, fish, and even guns.

1965. I MADE T-SHIRTS THAT JUST FLIPPED OUT AT THE BOTTOM. BETSEY. xox

Some of my original Paraphernalia sketches done in crayon. I loved how angular girls were in the 1960s, a body type I admired but never had at the time.

1966. xox BETSEY.

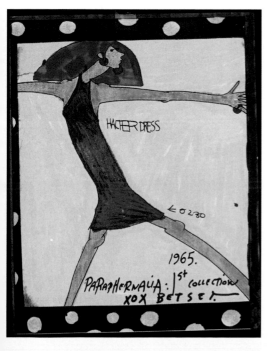

HACTER DRESS

←0230

1965.
PARAPHERNALIA: 1st COLLECTION
XOX BETSEY.

Sketches for the murals that covered the walls of my stores. I had graduated to colored markers by this point, and you can see clearly how my style evolved with the times. The girls got sexier and *way* more voluptuous.

print guy in the graphics department who had the tough job of turning it into a repeat pattern. I had to learn to ignore the look of shock and dread on his face when he saw the amount of detail in my drawings! Better him than me, since this was the process I hated so much back in school.

The work was all done by hand on graph paper. Each little square on the paper represented a stitch to the knitting machines. Because this was very complicated sweater work, it was a tedious process. It could take the poor guy up to two weeks to complete just one design before it was ready to go to the knitting factory in North Philly, which at the time was the unofficial knitting capital of the world.

I always brought the completed designs to the factory in person because I wanted to oversee the production process and make sure everything was running smoothly. In fact, I ended up spending so much time in North Philly that I almost took an apartment there, but instead stayed in crappy little motels right off the highway. I'd go back and forth from the factory to the motel, sleeping for two hours whenever I could. It wasn't glamorous but it was all part of the job.

The machines ran day and night, and the crew at the factory worked on them around the clock. The other reason I insisted on being there alongside the factory workers was that I wanted them to see how important this work was to me. And that was the right decision. I've always felt an affinity with people who worked with their hands, or in this case, the big knitting machines. Even though they were machinists, they worked with the precision of artisans. Eventually I formed a bond with the workers, and this made a big difference in how they handled my designs.

It was a hassle, but if the knitting machines missed even one stitch, an entire run could be ruined. Luckily, this rarely happened. The result was an item that even though it was manufactured on a machine, still had a handmade feel to it, which I felt people at that time wanted and appreciated.

For some of my other designs I traveled much farther than dreary North Philly. I was about to see whole other chunks of the world, which would prove to be wildly eye opening and exciting. Outside of going to London with *Mademoiselle* and my ninety-nine-dollar weekend excursions to Puerto Rico, I had never really traveled anywhere.

One of the first countries I visited was India, which I loved right from my very first trip there. It was *the* place to go for wovens, so lots of people were producing fabrics there. (In fact, ironically, I would often run into my predecessor Willi Smith, which was crazy, as he lived down the street from me in New York, but I never saw him in our neighborhood.) I was so excited to see what they had to show me that I couldn't wait to get to the textile factory. After an eighteen-hour flight it took me awhile to get a taxi—you haven't lived until you've taken a taxi in India—and when I finally arrived, I was frazzled and surprised to see that the production facility wasn't a factory at all. The setup was more like a series of small huts.

As soon as I got out of the taxi I was greeted by the workers, who were all women. Each one was intricately wrapped up in a beautiful sari woven in the most intense colors. I don't know if it has something to do with the quality of the light in that part of the world, but believe me when I tell you, they are not afraid of color. I felt as if I was being greeted by a bunch of beautifully wrapped gifts. I didn't speak the language but I could tell they were happy to see me and eager to show me what they were working on.

One of the women took me by the hand and then the group led me through the cramped workrooms and out to the back. I was not prepared for the surreal landscape that greeted me.

As far as the eye could see, freshly dyed yarns hung drying in the hot, glaring Indian sun.

Draped in the branches of the trees were my most extreme oranges and yellows and reds. It looked as though the trees were on fire. Across the grass stretched cobalt blues and bright greens. Between this explosion of color, the suffocating heat, the nauseating cab ride, and the long flight I felt as if I was going to faint and had to sit down. All the little wrapped gifts thought this was funny and laughed their heads off.

Over the next two weeks I continued to be mesmerized and impressed by the amazing craftsmanship of these women. Every bit done by hand in conditions that were way beyond rustic. I mean, they were dragging miles of wet yarn, which must have weighed a hundred pounds, down to the river to rinse off the dyes. Once the yarns were rinsed and dried we started the weaving process—or, I should say, they did. I watched them, completely spellbound as their nimble hands danced across the huge looms, creating the patterns I had designed. Inch by inch, foot by foot, and eventually yard by yard I saw my visions come to life.

But India wasn't all sunshine, incense, and spicy food. There was a man there who worked as a contractor and acted as an agent between Alley Cat and the factories. He took care of the business end of things. I will refer to him as "the great white hunter" as he wore only white clothing. I assume he thought I was also involved in the business end of things, because he would not leave me alone. Every night I had to fend off his advances as he tried repeatedly to get into the tent where I was staying in lieu of a hotel. I wanted to be close to the factory, and this was the easiest solution. I had to lock the zipper tight on my tent room, and even then he would harass me until I fell asleep.

I also traveled to Turkey, where we weren't producing fabrics, we were purchasing existing textiles. The factories in Turkey could not have been more different than the ones I visited in India.

When I first got there, after my experience in India, I expected to see more rustic conditions but I was pleasantly surprised when I walked through the door of a nondescript, dingy industrial-looking building. Once inside my preconceived perceptions were completely blown away. It wasn't like being in a factory at all. It was like stepping into a space capsule or some kind of a lab. Everything was meticulous and sterile with all the workers dressed in white. I was met by the manager of the facility, who spoke English.

While giving me a tour, he explained that the factory was responsible for manufacturing government-issued pajamas. He showed me pretty florals, which were the women's, and great stripes, which were the men's. I remember being amused that garments produced for the government would be so beautifully designed. I fell in love with the prints, and my creative juices started to flow. I immediately had a hundred ideas about what I wanted to do with them.

When I wasn't at the factories or my hotel, I toured the city on my own. I foolishly thought it was okay for a young American girl to go out and about alone. I made that mistake only once. I was doing some sightseeing and wanted to do it like the locals, so I got on a crowded bus filled mostly with men. It was very hot. All of the men were wearing traditional Turkish robes that reached the floor.

Standing in the middle of this mob, I started to feel hands all over me. It began slowly with the bus jostling as it rode over unpaved streets. I attributed the men bumping into me to the bad roads. But then I felt more and more men bumping up and down on me and I got the idea pretty quickly. I jumped off the bus at the next stop. I never made that mistake again!

Detained in Dubrovnik

I had memorable experiences in all of the countries I traveled to, but nothing beats what happened to me in Yugoslavia.

After one of my trips to India, I planned to go to London by way of Belgrade, where I wanted to spend a couple of days. I usually got one of my boyfriends to meet me on these side trips, but for this one I couldn't scare up any of them, so I was traveling alone. The flight from India to Belgrade was supposed to take something like ten hours, which I wasn't looking forward to. I always hated those long flights, but I did love the time off after a long, strenuous work trip.

After we were in the air for what seemed like forever, the crew made an announcement saying we'd be landing in Dubrovnik. They never explained the change in destination but just apologized for the inconvenience blah, blah, blah. Part of me didn't care. I was dying to get off that plane.

We exited right on the runway, and the crew lined us all up. It was the middle of the night, and it was cold, which felt good after the extreme heat I had been experiencing for two weeks in India. They asked everyone to show their passports, and one by one everyone did. I couldn't imagine what was going on. I thought maybe someone on the plane was a criminal or something.

When they got to me, they looked at my passport, then at me, and seemed alarmed. They eyed me suspiciously, then pulled me aside and had me wait away from the other passengers.

I was starting to get nervous. Did I look suspicious? Had I been mistaken for a spy?

When they finally finished checking everyone's passports, I realized I was the only person they had singled out. Now all of the other passengers were eyeing me funny.

If I was nervous before, I was shocked now, as they started to let everyone back on board except me. I stared paralyzed as the plane started taxiing down the runway and then watched it take off in slow motion and disappear into the night. I was left there with some official from the airline who wouldn't listen to me as I begged him to tell me what was going on. He wouldn't even look at me. I wracked my brain trying to figure out what I could possibly have done to deserve this treatment.

All of a sudden, seemingly out of nowhere, a white van came screaming toward us. It stopped, and two guys got out wearing white smocks, skull caps, and surgical masks. They were accompanied by two policemen who had their guns drawn.

Had I lost my mind? I was literally about to be dragged away by men in white coats!

They put me in the back of the van, which looked like a cross between an ambulance and a paddy wagon. It was all very white and scary.

We took off, but they drove at normal speed, and there was no siren. I was alone in the back but could see the police and the white-coat guys through a screen that separated me from them.

We drove for I don't know how long. I just sat there in stunned silence, feeling that I shouldn't make a sound.

We finally arrived at some kind of clinic or hospital. It was very strange—a small building surrounded by a high wall with an armed guard at the gate.

As they unloaded me out of the back of the van, I noticed that the white-coat guys were now wearing rubber gloves as they pushed me toward the back door of the building. The sun was just starting to come up as the door slammed shut.

They marched me down some long, clinical-smelling hallways, the whole time speaking in that harsh Slavic language I didn't understand. It just all sounded scary and mean. At the end of the hall they pushed me into a room with an examining table, a couple of chairs, and an uncomfortable-looking cot. Everything was lit by bright fluorescent lights and smelled of disinfectant. I immediately started to think of it as my jail cell.

After about an hour, without a knock, the door burst open, and one of the masked attendants, a policeman, and a woman came in. The woman was dressed like the attendant, in a white lab coat. She was very eastern European looking, with thin lips, high heels, and a clipboard. She reminded me of Lotte Lenya in *From Russia with Love*. She was very stern and started to ask me questions in Yugoslavian, even though I was sure she knew I was American, and the attendants must have told her I didn't speak the language.

She said something to one of them, and he approached me with a hypodermic needle. Well, that was *it*. While I had previously been quiet, submissive, and basically in shock, I now flipped. And when I say I flipped, I mean, I went wild! I started screaming and shouting and flailing my arms. I was so scared of that needle and can't imagine what they were trying to shoot me up with. I went so crazy that they all left the room, slamming the door behind them, leaving me alone, hyperventilating.

After about half an hour there was a light knock on the door, and another woman came in. This one looked like a peasant and was also wearing a surgical mask and holding a basket. She reached inside and handed me two boiled hot dogs. She seemed much nicer than all the other people I'd encountered so far. I took the food from her and thanked her. She removed the mask and smiled a toothless smile and then turned around and left.

I gobbled up the two hot dogs. I hadn't realized how hungry I was. My last meal had been when I first boarded the plane the day before. After eating, I curled up on the cot in a fetal position and actually managed to fall asleep.

When I finally opened my eyes, I realized I must have been

asleep for a while and that someone had come in and left blankets and some water and finally turned off those horrible fluorescent lights. I got under the covers. I couldn't imagine what would happen next.

After what seemed like hours there was another rap on the door, and the pleasant peasant lady was back with my breakfast of two more boiled hot dogs. After she left, From Russia with Love was back with her clipboard and more Slavic questions that I couldn't answer. She seemed really angry and left in a huff.

A short time later the peasant woman returned and indicated that I should come with her. She took me back out through those harshly lit corridors. It was very quiet, and there didn't seem to be anyone else around. She led me outside, I assumed to get some air.

The clinic, or whatever it was, was actually situated in a beautiful location right on a hill overlooking what I now realize must have been the Adriatic Sea. I was able to appreciate how beautiful the setting was in spite of my circumstances. The day was much warmer than the night had been and I started to calm down a little. I even managed to communicate a bit with the peasant woman. She spoke no English but did nod when I asked her if I was in a hospital. When I asked her if she knew why, she only shrugged. Her toothless smile was oddly comforting.

I tried to scope out the scene in the hospital yard. There was the guardhouse I had seen when they brought me in. An old man was in it, but he was sitting in a chair and looked to be sleeping. When I saw his gun resting against the wall, it didn't seem as threatening as it had the night before.

We walked around for a while in the sun, and I began feeling better and thinking more clearly.

In fact, I came up with a plan: I would escape. And without giving it much more thought, I got away from the peasant woman and past the guardhouse easily enough. I ran down the hill as fast as I could, turned a corner, and saw an open-sided old bus coming down the street. I sped after it and managed to jump on, and in about ten minutes we pulled into the bus station. I found the nearest phone booth, got in, and closed the door behind me. I swear I could hear my heart pounding. I tried to figure out how to place a person-to-person international call to my boyfriend in New York but I kept getting a Yugoslavian operator on the line who didn't understand me. I was crying into the receiver saying, "Please, please help me!" Then I heard a knock on the phone booth door. I turned and saw it was a policeman.

I went quietly with him. He brought me, not surprisingly, back to the clinic. I was really scared now. I was sure they were going to rough me up for running away. It was a nightmare!

When they brought me back into my room, there were more people there than before, including a tall, good-looking man who reminded me of Omar Sharif. He spoke to me in broken English, at first apologizing, and then started explaining why I'd been brought there.

He told me there had been a cholera epidemic in India for over ten years. During that time many countries hadn't allowed flights from India to land. Yugoslavia was one of them. It had relaxed its restrictions a bit now that the epidemic seemed to be over but still took precautions like double-checking anyone who was coming into the country from India.

Which is what happened at the airport. I had had all my shots, like I was supposed to. The trouble was, the person who inspected my passport at the airport in India didn't check the right boxes or something, and my paperwork didn't gibe with the fact that I had indeed been inoculated.

So there you go: enter the men in the white coats and surgical masks. Apparently there were no patients at the clinic, so it was closed for the weekend. When the head doctor, whom I was speaking to now, couldn't be reached, From Russia with Love, who was the second in command, had to be called in in the middle of her Saturday night and she was not happy about it. So that explained her nasty behavior. She had been trying to explain to me, in Yugoslavian, that all they needed to do was give me my shots and keep me there for a couple of days to make sure I was okay.

But I flipped out, screamed, and ran. As for the hot dog lady, she was a cleaning woman and was just sharing her lunch with me because she knew there was no food kept at the clinic!

They made some phone calls and somehow eventually cleared up the mystery of whether or not I had had my shots.

The doctor now asked me if I wanted to get out of the country. "Yes!" I said, bursting into tears. "Yes! I want to go home!" I felt like Dorothy at the end of *The Wizard of Oz*.

They got my luggage, which I hadn't even realized had come with me from the airport.

The two attendants and I went to the train station together and they waited until my train took off. I guess they wanted to make sure I was really gone. Lesson: Know that if you get held up in *any* country, you can leave on the *very* next train, plane, or anything. They have to let you go if they have no proof of wrongdoing.

At the airport, a ticket to New York City was waiting for me at the Pan Am desk. I was never so happy to get on a plane in my life, and as we were landing I just kept saying, "There's no place like home! There's no place like home!"

Back to Reality

After my first year with Alley Cat, I more than proved myself and managed to deliver on the promises I'd made when they took me on . . . and then some.

The company did more than $5 million in sales, and my designs were well received by the press. Life in the fickle world of fashion can be tricky at best. I loved my work situation and was eager for it to continue. I was now twenty-eight years old and was feeling the need for the first time for some financial security.

I decided to ask Leonard for a four-year contract. I went to his office in North Philly and was surprised, but not really, when he agreed to my request. He was a smart businessman who knew a good thing when he saw it. His company was doing big numbers without his having to lift a finger. He told me to keep doing what I was doing and then shocked me by telling me he was also giving me a car as a bonus. I went straight to a car dealership and got myself a 500CC Bentley motorbike! They also raised my salary to three hundred dollars a week.

I had played my hand just right and it paid off.

In 1971, two years into working for Alley Cat—that is, two very *successful* years, which actually means four very well-received seasons—I learned I was to be given the coveted Coty Award that September. This was like being told you had just won an Oscar. I couldn't imagine how I was even in consideration for such a prestigious award. I had no clue as to how those things were run. I later found out that Edie Locke, good old Edie, had nominated me. I couldn't believe it! And, as I heard through the grapevine, neither could a number of other people in the fashion industry—I will not name names (Donna Karan, Diane von Furstenberg). They were riled, as they didn't think of me as a *real* fashion designer. I was someone who designed clothes for a clothing manufacturer. Apparently in some people's minds there is a difference.

I was to receive the award alongside Halston. Anne Klein and Bill Blass were receiving lesser awards. I was in major good company here. I called my mom and dad right away and told them that they *had* to come to the ceremony. Even though it was to be held in their dreaded New York City.

The worst part of that night was what I looked like. I had intended to wear my hair long, loose, and curly, but it would not cooperate, and at the last minute I ended up putting it into braids and pinning it to the top of my head, which is how I wore it for work. And for some reason I decided to wear a tuxedo that I'd designed. It was black velvet with a big black-velvet bowtie. It was *so* not me and I felt uncomfortable all night. I guess I wanted to look more important and grown-up than I felt. I knew the place would be packed with all the fashion heavy hitters, and it was.

The ceremony was held at Parsons School of Design. It was a big, boring dinner. In fact, the whole affair was very stuffy and very fashion establishment. They took everything *so* seriously, which is another reason it had been such a shock to people, me included, that I had won.

Halston and I represented high end and low end, respectively.

I actually wound up meeting one of my all-time fashion idols, the man best known as the inventor of the topless bathing suit, Rudi Gernreich. I couldn't imagine how they had gotten him to attend. He was notorious for being a bit of a hermit

Daddy, Leonard Shandal, me, and Mom at the Coty Awards

and didn't make a lot of public appearances. Besides, he lived on the West Coast, and I had heard that he rarely came east.

I approached him at his table and told him briefly how much

I admired his work. He was a small, quiet man and nodded, thanked me, said how much he loved my work, and I walked away.

The only part of my own acceptance speech I remember is that I know I called out the fact that, at twenty-nine, I was the youngest person ever, even to this day, to receive the award. I spoke a little about how important it was to recognize young talent. I acknowledged Edie Locke and Mary Lou Luther, the fashion editor of the *Los Angeles Times*, as two women who had championed me from the start of my career. I knew that my winning was just as big a coup for them as it was for me. I often refer to them as my fashion fairy godmothers, because without their support I would never have been living this fairy tale.

The speeches were dull, but at least there were fashion presentations from all of the honorees. This had given me something to focus on to take my mind off the enormity of getting the award. I was up first. There was no budget, so I used my girlfriends and friends of friends—anyone who fit the clothes—as my models. They did their own hair and makeup. I went all out, full tilt. I showed sweaters, embroidery, prairie dresses. I was all over the place. I did the announcements and commentary. Our table was right in front, and I could tell from the looks on my parents' faces how proud they were of me.

Halston was up next, and of course he dragged out all the Halstonettes: Pat Cleveland, Anjelica Huston, Karen Bjornson, Pat Ast. I don't quite remember how my ragtag friends and

Halston's all-star team got along backstage but I'm sure it was interesting.

To me, that time marked the final days of independent expression. It was a time before you had to be a dear friend of Anna Wintour or Japanese or have a lot of money and a big corporation behind you to get recognized.

About a week before the ceremony, I went to Leonard Shandal and threw some of my newfound weight around. This was a pretty big honor for a label like Alley Cat—unprecedented, even. I told him he just had to throw me a party after the award ceremony, and he did. It was at Tavern on the Green, and I insisted they hire Ray Barretto and his band to perform. I loved going to El Corso on the Upper East Side on Saturday nights to see Ray perform and to salsa dance with my girlfriends. So it was a no-brainer who I wanted to perform at my party.

I went with my parents to Tavern on the Green directly from Parsons. I couldn't wait for the fun part of the evening to start. When I walked in, the party was already in full swing. Ray was set up with his band but they were playing what sounded like elevator music and not his usual high-energy salsa.

I didn't know Ray personally but I went right to the bandstand, reached up, and tugged on the hem of the outrageous velvet blazer he was wearing to get his attention. When he looked down at me, I said to him, "Hey, Ray, what's going on? You're gonna put everyone to sleep. This is the biggest night of my life, it's supposed to be a party!" He stopped the band and the boring music and told me that Leonard had instructed them to cool it. "Well, it's my party," I said, "and *I'm* telling you to do what you do. And play it loud!" Things picked up after that. My parents even danced.

There were probably about three hundred people in the room. I had no idea who many of them were. Most likely they were fashion industry types, Leonard's garmento cronies, and some press people. In spite of my hair disaster and questionable outfit, I managed to have a magical night.

As usual, the next day Cinderella was back to reality and at work, bright and early.

The next few seasons continued to be successful, but there was an eventual slowdown. They say the first three years on a job are telling. The first year you're in the honeymoon phase: you've just been hired, and the bosses believe they made the right decision, so it's all good. The second year you find your groove and keep going. The third year you're kinda trying to keep it fresh. This is where I was now, and it wasn't good.

I could still continue doing what I was doing, which was making more cutesy things. Things that I still loved to wear. But the business was starting to change—not just at Alley Cat but in the world of fashion as a whole. The junior market, which I was so good at designing, was evolving. Fashion was growing up, and the trend now was to a more minimal style of dressing. This change in attitude provided an opportunity for people like Calvin Klein and Donna Karan to make their mark. Styles

With Pat Cleveland and Norma Jean Darden—Spring 1974
Ready-to-Wear Collection

Alley Cat Spring 1973 runway show with Daddy Rabbit

were getting more sophisticated and more minimal and that sure wasn't me! I did give it a go . . . once. I had a couple of beautiful three-piece linen suits made for me in Hong Kong, but of course I never ended up wearing them. I gave them to my sister.

For the first time since I started at Alley Cat, our sales were down, and Leonard was getting jumpy.

He wanted the clothes to get with the times and be more trend driven and I guess more grown-up. He also wanted to be involved with what I was doing. I have never followed trends, and didn't intend to start now.

I did not like it one bit, but my contract had more than a year left on it. I tried to design the things that Norman wanted, but they were *so* not me. I did a couple of wrap dresses, which I had done before, but he wanted them in boring and what I considered to be ugly colors, and less expensive fabrics, which to me felt sleazy and cheap looking.

I tried to explain to him that certain shapes required certain fabrications to make them work. I knew he understood, but at the same time he didn't care. He'd been in the business for years. He may have been a garmento but he was also a good businessman and he was looking at the bottom line. He had nothing to lose. After all, it wasn't his name on the label.

I gave it my all but my spirit was crushed. If I wanted to leave Alley Cat, I knew I'd have to buy my way out of the remainder of my contract, which I was sure was the right move.

It would get me *out* of the spotlight, *out* of the drive, drive, drive. So in 1974 I approached Leonard and told him I wanted out of our deal, that I couldn't fake it anymore. He agreed, and that was that. I left, on good terms of course.

Maybe it wasn't the best decision I could have made at that moment because I had also made another life-changing decision. I decided that it was time to have a baby.

7.) A SINGLE MOTHER.

Back in the 1970s, single motherhood had a couple of things in common with PMS. We didn't have a name for it yet, and people thought of it as either a horrible fate or a psychological issue. Today having a baby without having a husband is not such a big deal, but back then it just wasn't a *thing*.

In 1973 I was dating a guy named Joe. He was an artist. Not a successful artist, mind you, though I think he was a pretty good one. He made large metal sculptures, and whenever I think of him—which is as infrequently as humanly possible—I always picture him wearing one of those big, scary welding masks.

I don't know what the attraction was, because he was a very cold person. "Icy" is the only way

I can think to describe him. In spite of that, or maybe because of that, I was always trying to find out what made him tick, to crack him. I think I had a Florence Nightingale complex, always trying to save the men I dated. And who knows, maybe I even looked for men who needed saving.

I met Joe just walking down the street one day. I was coming out of the Strand bookstore and I saw this super-skinny tall guy. I have always been attracted to guys like that, and this one was wiry like a pipe cleaner. We started talking, and he asked me about the books I had just bought. They were all vintage children's books. I was designing a line of children's clothing at the time and used the antique illustrations as references. Joe seemed into me and before I knew what was happening he invited me to his loft to see his work. That's not my idea of a typical date, but the next afternoon I went over and I watched him cut and weld large metal pieces together. I was fascinated. Sparks were flying all over the place, literally and figuratively. I've always loved watching passionate people at work, especially the men I dated.

Joe's studio was nearby my tiny fourth-floor walk-up apartment on Eleventh Street, right off Fifth Avenue. After a couple of weeks I gave up my place and moved in with him. I don't know why I moved in with guys so quickly. I was such a romantic and have always believed in love at first sight. In this case, I was at Joe's studio so much that moving in seemed like the obvious thing to do. Also, it cut our total rent in half, since my apartment had cost $250 a month, the same as his loft.

It was a *lot* of space for so little money. And it was *raw*. Joe had metal plates installed on the floors to support the weight. He had some art collectors from Texas who commissioned his work. There were pulleys and winches hanging from the ceiling, and the air always had a burnt metallic smell to it. We slept in a bed in the farthest corner away from where he did his work. It was the only place I've ever lived that I didn't decorate or at least try to make homey. Believe me, a pair of lace curtains or a bright paint job wouldn't have helped. It was *not* that kind of space.

So I was kind of happy to be traveling for some of my free-lance gigs that I was now doing instead of being tied down to one company. I spent a lot of time in Hong Kong, which is also where I had produced some of my clothes for Alley Cat. I would visit factories, source fabrics, and oversee production, and some-times I was even able to get some shopping in, as well as a glimpse of the exotic sights and sounds of the city.

At times I was away for as long as six weeks. These over-seas trips could be exhausting, but it was coming back to the loft that became harder and harder as Joe and I started to drift apart. It got so that I would dread that four-flight climb up-stairs with all my bags and God knows what else I dragged back with me—only to open the door to that burning metal smell and not even a "Welcome home."

Despite our relationship going off track, I got pregnant. A baby certainly wasn't what Joe wanted in his life, but it was what *I* wanted. I was thirty-three years old at the time and I figured if I was ever going to have a baby, I'd better get on with it. For my whole life I'd always known that I wanted a kid.

Circumstances may not have been ideal, but once I found out I was pregnant, nothing else mattered—including what Joe thought about it. I couldn't be sure of anything else in my life. I couldn't be sure of having a man or money, even though I was then doing all right for myself financially. There was plenty of work, and I was in demand. As far as not being certain of having a man around, I didn't care. Nothing else mattered except that I wanted this baby. Nothing was going to stop me from having it. And that included my resolve to not marry Joe.

I was excited to tell my parents, but was also worried about how they were going to take the news. They lived in a very small, conservative Connecticut town, and I figured they'd have to deal with some backlash from their neighbors about my not being married. You know how it goes: people *will* talk. And I had no intention of being discreet about my pregnancy—I was going to keep going home for visits, no matter how big and obvious I got.

In fact my parents were always very "go with the flow." Things might rile them at first, but they were ultimately always supportive of me and my brother and sister. I wasn't scared to tell them I was pregnant, but I was biding my time, getting used to the idea myself. Then one day I picked up the phone and called my mother and just said, "Mom, guess what?" And I told her. She was quiet at first and then said, "Oh, how nice," or something benign like that. There were a few questions: How far along are you? How are you feeling? Have you thought about a name? Is it a boy or a girl?

But oddly enough there were no questions about Joe. They'd met him only a couple of times, but that was enough for him to make a negative impression. Joe couldn't have been less charming when I dragged him home to Connecticut or when my parents made a rare trip to New York. Whether he was sitting on my parents' couch or at the table with them at a restaurant in the city, he would cross his arms and go all sullen, barely saying a word. I swear, in my mind's eye he pulled on his welding mask any time my parents were in the room. I think my parents would definitely have preferred that I was married to the baby's father, but I'd like to think they were secretly glad that I didn't marry Joe.

My mother then changed the subject and started to update me on her world. We hung up, and that was it. It went exactly as I imagined it would. After I'd made it clear that I wasn't ever going to marry Joe—especially for the sake of the baby—there was silence. That was certainly better than their arguing with me or being passive aggressive. They kept their negative thoughts to themselves, thank God.

But as casual as Mom was at first, in the weeks and months

that followed both she and my father started getting used to the idea of my becoming a mother. They were excited at the notion of becoming grandparents again. My sister already had three kids, and my brother two, having gotten a much earlier start than I did. I think the whole family had given up any hope that I would *ever* have a baby.

One thing they didn't stay silent about was the name I'd already chosen for her: Lulu. Oh God, they hated that name! They associated it with a woman of, shall I say, loose morals? Lulu was a character in a little ditty my dad used to play for us on the piano when we were kids. The lyrics went something like this . . . *"If you're coming to the party—you can bring Kate or you can bring Nate but don't bring Lulu."* (These are the G-rated lyrics.) An odd song to be singing around the living room after dinner, to be sure. But we kids didn't know what it meant, so it was funny.

The real inspiration for the name I'd chosen came from some friends who had just gotten back from Mexico and brought me a little statue of the Virgin of Guadalupe. I fell in love with the name Guadalupe, which I had never heard before, and even more, its shortened form, Lulu. Also, Little Lulu had always been my favorite cartoon character. I loved her hair and her little red A-line dress with the Peter Pan collar! Plus, she showed her panties a lot and was kinda naughty, and that had appealed to me as a little girl.

No matter how many times I told my parents where I got

the name, they just couldn't get past the woman in that dirty little song! It's funny that it never occurred to me to choose a boy's name. It never *once* crossed my mind that there was a fifty-fifty chance that I might have a boy. Thank God I had a girl, what would I *ever* have done with a boy?!

Real trouble started between Joe and me around the seventh or eighth month of my pregnancy. Before then it was just minor annoyances, but by then everything was blowing up all out of proportion, and I was nearly ready for him to just disappear. I couldn't stand the sight of him anymore.

I had finally become convinced he was never going to change. I knew he wasn't going to lift a finger to help financially with the baby. I knew he wasn't going to get a *job* job—a real paying one. In my view, he was too much into the mystique of the starving artist. There were the odd commissions here and there, but no steady contribution to the household. Until then I used to say to him, "You know, even Benjamin Franklin worked at the post office!" I thought, *Just bring home a steady hundred dollars a week. Something. Anything.* All I wanted was for him to try, but no. I was the one making sure all the bills got paid and the lights stayed on. I was going to be responsible for baby Lulu and I wanted him to go.

I didn't give much thought to the logistics of single motherhood. I just knew it had to be a whole lot easier without daddy around if mommy and daddy weren't happy. And mommy and daddy were *not* happy. So forget it. Get it over with. Too many people say, "We gotta stay together for the kids." Blah, blah, blah, meanwhile, they're fooling around on each other; they don't like who they've become; they're lying, and not only to each other, but to *themselves.*

As I got used to the idea of raising a kid alone—and believe me, I still had some doubts as to *how* I was going to do it—a memory came back to me. In 1968 I was in the Amazon jungle with Hideoki, my photographer boyfriend at the time. I was sent there by Braniff Airlines as part of a promotion for tourism in Peru. The tagline they were planning on using went something like "We love Peru. We believe in Peru. Let's see if these people love Peru, too." Bill Blass was also along for the trip. I guess Peru was targeting a fashion customer.

It was a pretty fun gig. They flew us all expenses paid for a week in Lima, a week in Cuzco, and a week in the Amazon. We posed for photos all along the way for their PR, which was easy. The only tough part would be meeting with the Braniff executives at the end of the trip to share our impressions of the country. I would have to tell them that I couldn't possibly promote tourism in Peru. It was too beautiful, too real, too perfect. Tourism would ruin it. Not what they wanted to hear at all.

Anyway, while we were in Peru, along the Amazon River, I saw a native Indian couple walking down to the water, dragging a canoe behind them. The woman was topless and looked to be in the last stages of pregnancy. They were both wearing loincloths, but I couldn't see hers, because her belly was so big.

The man put the canoe in the water and then very gently helped the woman sit in it. I thought to myself, *Oh, isn't this a nice little authentic Amazonian moment I'm witnessing.* And then I saw him give the canoe a shove, and off she went down the river *alone*! I said to Hideoki, "Can you believe that?" It looked as if he was dumping her. I was shocked. But two days later I saw the same woman walking through the village, carrying a newborn baby.

That little seed of an image got embedded somewhere in my brain. And now, so many years later, it came floating to the surface, and I thought, *If that woman could* give birth *alone in the middle of the Amazon, then I could certainly* raise *a baby alone in the middle of Manhattan.* I had made up my mind what I wanted to do.

Right before the baby was born, I told Joe that as soon as I was strong enough after the delivery, I wanted to move out with Lulu. He immediately threatened me. I wasn't expecting that. He said that if I left, he'd break into my apartment in the middle of the night and take the baby away. I knew he didn't want a child, so I assumed he wanted to hold on to me as his meal ticket. I couldn't be sure. I was absolutely frantic. Would he really resort to kidnapping?

My due date was April 7, which just so happened to be the day of the fashion show for the children's line that I was producing as another one of my seemingly endless freelance gigs. I remember telling the very jumpy clothing manufacturers

Popping out a baby and a children's line at the same time!

who were backing it, "Don't worry. I'm not having this kid on my due date. It's not gonna happen." I swore to them up and down. I simply couldn't have the kid right then. I was in rehearsal, counting down to the show. I was still sewing, very rapidly, keeping my legs and fingers crossed!

On the morning of the show, I'd gone for my last ob-gyn exam to find out exactly how much longer I had to go. Believe it or not, they told me right then on my due date that I was having twins! Now that really knocked my socks off.

From the doctor's office I went directly to do the show, which was at a famous old New York City restaurant. It was an upscale, fancy ice cream parlor in the Garment District. I cannot for the life of me remember the name of the place.

It was similar to Serendipity 3, where I used to hang out with the Warhol crowd.

Right as the show was about to start I looked at all the kids lined up to walk the runway. I tried to imagine twice as many of them. Could I get used to having two babies instead of just the one that I was prepared for? There was no time to process that possibility. I had bigger fish to fry at the moment.

The show went off without a hitch and without my going into labor. When I came out onstage at the finale, I was wearing a yellow and white-striped T-shirt under my yellow empire waist corduroy jumper with a "Back to School" embroidered patch on the pocket and little puff sleeves. It was an adult version of one of the pieces in the show. The audience audibly gasped. They'd never seen me pregnant, and let me tell you, I was *huge*. But it worked to my advantage. There was something very *real* about a woman in the full bloom of pregnancy doing a line of children's clothes.

The very next morning I went out to pick up a newspaper, and BOOM! I knew I had to go to the hospital right away. I grabbed Joe from his studio, and we found a cab to Beth Israel. Sitting in the back of the car, struggling with my contractions, I had to smile that we had given up on the Lamaze method. We'd discovered that I could never sit still long enough . . . let alone *breathe*. So that went out the window pretty early on in the pregnancy, which turned out to be a good thing, because now that my water had actually broken, I couldn't stand the idea of Joe touching me.

As soon as we got to the hospital, the doctors gave me Pitocin to help things along. Ten hours went by, and still no baby. By then it was getting close to ten thirty, and they were preparing to give me an epidural. Next thing I know, WHAM! Out comes Lulu. Just like that! I didn't have time for the needle. I had no intention of going natural, but I did. And just one baby, hallelujah! To this day I don't know how the doctor messed up by telling me that I was having twins.

But there she was, my beautiful, perfect baby, Lulu. I was just *so* happy and *so* relieved. I knew I had my ultimate best girlfriend. Joe was there at the birth, wearing a mask, but didn't participate in any way. It was the classic male thing. I don't

My favorite picture of me and Lulu

remember him even holding the baby. My first words to Lulu were, "It's just me and you against the world, babe."

The next day Joe was out the door to Mexico, where he had a small commission. I didn't have much time for recovery, because I had a show for yet another freelance gig that week. And true to my word, I was also packing to move out of the loft.

I didn't tell Joe where we were going, but he found out somehow. Late one night when Lulu's nanny was still with me at my new third-floor apartment, she screamed. Looking out the window, we could see Joe trying to scale the building like Spiderman. I let out a scream, too, and then Lulu started screaming.

Well, that scared him away, but I didn't sleep a wink all night. If he was willing to scale the outside of a New York City apartment building, there was no telling what else he might do. I guess I underestimated how crazy he was. The next day I went to the police station and took out a restraining order. Joe wasn't to come within twenty feet of me or Lulu.

He didn't attempt anything like that again, and shortly after, I heard through the grapevine that he'd left the city. I never quite believed he was gone, and that we were completely safe. Sometimes I'd think I saw him on the street, and my heart would race. I'd duck into the nearest doorway, but it never turned out to be him. I was just living with that kind of fear.

A couple of years later I got a call from a woman who said that she was Joe's wife. She told me that she wanted me to support Joe, her, and *their four children*. I must have developed a much stronger constitution by this time because I broke into hysterical laughter and hung up on her. I never heard from them again.

From the first moment, it was just Lulu and me. I took her everywhere. I nursed her through meeting after meeting with clients. I never thought twice about it. I'd excuse myself and go to the bathroom. People pretty quickly got used to me showing up with Lulu and they loved her. I was just so comfortable with her, and she was such a good baby. I still took care of business first, but now I did it all with Lulu on my hip.

My freelance work was keeping me busier and busier. So much so that at one point I was designing different products for about nine clients: hosiery for Capezio, lingerie for a company called Mistee, shoes for I. Miller and Nina, sportswear and jeans for Adriana Goldschmidt, T-shirts for Michael Millet, to name a few. I was all over the place and so busy! Eventually I did need help with Lulu and I must have gone through at least five babysitters before I found Ada Potata. That's the nickname that made Lulu laugh.

Ada Potata would take Lulu to her Baptist church in Harlem every Sunday and would sometimes travel with us to Hong Kong when I needed to have Lulu with me. Lulu loved her, and their bond made it possible, when Lulu was only three years old, for me to open my own showroom. This was a major move. I was going to have my own line—one that I designed, produced, and controlled myself. But I couldn't work from home anymore. So Ada stayed with Lulu. It was the first time Lulu and I were apart all day, every day. The separation anxiety devastated me. When I wasn't with Lulu, it felt like a part of me was missing.

But I couldn't take her everywhere once I started my business. I also relied on my next-door neighbor, Keni Valenti, an amazing vintage dealer and an early Barbie doll collector. He was a complete insomniac. When I wanted to go out to the Mudd Club, which was just three blocks away, Keni would settle in at one of my sewing machines to make Barbie clothes all night long while Lulu slept.

The Mudd Club was *the* crazy/creative–people getaway, and where I went to keep current—to see and be seen. It was the epicenter of the punk/new wave scene in New York City, more artsy fartsy than CBGB's. Keith Haring curated art shows, and there was live music every night. The Mudd Club was the after-hours continuation of my workday. It was my mid-1970s

Outside the Mudd Club with the one-of-a-kind Klaus Nomi and Kenny Scharf

Max's Kansas City. Without Keni's sewing addiction and his help with Lulu, I could not have ventured out to the clubs to see what people were doing and be inspired.

And then there were my parents, who were absolutely head over heels in love with Lulu, despite their early misgivings about her name. I once had to go to Asia for a month-long business trip to work with a factory that was weaving the most beautiful peasant-style fabric for me. My parents said that they'd be happy to take Lulu for that long. My father, in particular, was happy for the extra time with her. They had a special bond and were closer to each other than I've ever seen either one of them be to anyone else. Maybe Lulu was instinctively looking for a father figure. Who knows, but he was a godsend.

Otherwise it was usually just Lulu and me. I don't know how I did it. I could never think of myself as the kitchy-kitchy-coo type of mother, the kind who would tickle a baby under the chin and talk baby talk. From day one I always spoke to Lulu like an adult. I was a mother, but I wasn't very maternal—not the coddling type. There were times, especially when I was on deadline, that I had to let her cry herself to sleep on my cutting table.

I did have fun dressing Lulu up when she was a baby, and she loved it, too. What baby wouldn't love wearing all kinds of kooky outfits? I made her some real costume-y things, but I also bought her *really* expensive stuff. I remember dressing her in a lot of white—which I learned is a terrible idea for a baby! I spoiled her with clothes in a way I wouldn't spend money on

 Baby Lulu as Raggedy Ann with Aunt Sally and Mom

Lulu at five years old

my own wardrobe. I don't know why I acted like a rich grand-parent. I suppose I wanted to prove that I could provide for my baby girl all by myself.

As fate would have it, when Lulu started getting a little older, she had absolutely *no* interest in my clothes. As soon as she could choose her own outfits, all she ever wanted to wear were jeans and T-shirts and lots and lots of *gray*. She would never have been caught dead in pink!

Eight-year-old Lulu hated to be seen with me, because my purple leopard-print hair embarrassed her. She wanted nothing to do with my look. She'd actually try to walk on the other side of the street when we were out together. I was fine with that. She had the right to her feelings, just as I had the right to mine. But there was a lot of eye-rolling going on from both of us.

I somehow always knew that Lulu and I wouldn't live on different fashion planets forever. The apple can't fall *that* far from the tree! So I wasn't surprised that finally one day, when Lulu was fifteen years old and getting dressed to go out with her girlfriends, she chose a black bustier, miniskirt, fishnets, and high heels. I felt as if it was her way of telling me, "Maybe Mom isn't such a kook after all." I was so proud of the way she looked all dressed up to go out, and thought to myself, *That's my girl!*

8.) A WARDROBE IN STRETCH: GOING OUT ON MY OWN.

By 1977 I had been freelancing for almost four years, and it just wasn't doing the trick anymore. Even though I did have my name on some of the labels, it didn't feel like the real thing. I was getting tired of designing what was essentially someone else's vision.

One afternoon, while having a drink with my good friend, and favorite designer, Giorgio Sant'Angelo at Bill's Bar in the Garment District I was going on and on about how I felt as if I wasn't moving forward in my career. I was frustrated because I wanted to do what I wanted to do, and nobody seemed willing to hire me for that. He told me flat out, "Betsey, no one is going to do this *for* you. You need to do it for *yourself.* If I were you, I would just

design a line, plan a fashion show, and announce you're back."
Coming from Giorgio, this was a major statement. He was such
a gentle man, and I never saw him get his feathers ruffled. But
he seemed adamant about this, so he must have meant business.
Or he could have just been fed up with my complaining.

My fave, Giorgio Sant'Angelo, who told me to "Just do it!"

For at least a year I had been looking for a company that
would hire me and let me design my own line while they footed
the bill. I knew such companies existed because, up to a point,

that was the way things worked for me when I was at Alley Cat. Puritan, their parent company, owned a bunch of different labels, and each had its own designer. I only left Alley Cat when the label folks got too controlling, because I hated that feeling of being stifled. I had been spoiled at Paraphernalia. There I worked day and night, but I could make anything I wanted, as long as it sold. Lucky for me, it did.

I knew I still could *design* a line that would sell. But I thought taking on the business side as well would be overwhelming. When Giorgio dared me to stand on my own, I flashed back to six months earlier, when I had gone to see Frank Andrews, my favorite psychic. He said to me, "Betsey, why don't you just go to the beach and relax? You shouldn't be trying to start anything new at this point in time. It's simply not in the stars for you *right now*. Give yourself some time. Within six months I see you living in a new place and sporting a whole new look."

As Frank's words came back to me I realized the six-month waiting period was over. I should have taken his advice and just gone to the beach instead of beating myself up over my work situation. No wonder it hadn't felt right before. Now, I looked around my loft, which I had just painted hot pink and acid green, and realized that in effect I *was* living in a new space. I'd also cut off my curly brown hair, dyed it black, and wore it spiky and messy, like Keith Richards. My whole look had changed. So if Frank had been right about my living space and my appearance, maybe he was right about the future of my career as well.

Giorgio's real kick-in-the-pants advice, along with Frank's prediction, got me thinking in a whole different way. I had never really had to pursue jobs before. They had all more or less landed in my lap. Now I was finally going to take the lead and roll the dice. The more the idea of starting my own business sank in, the more excited I got. My gears were turning as I considered how to put the pieces together into a master plan.

I knew the first thing I would need was a partner in crime. There was no way I was going to do this alone. I immediately thought of my friend Chantal Bacon.

We'd met a few years earlier when she was the rep for the brief life of my Betsey Johnson Kids line. She did a great job of selling the line, so I knew she had that part down. Currently she was repping Cathy Hardwick's clothing line. As for the other business stuff, I wasn't so sure, and I suspected that it might be a challenge for her. I didn't get too hung up on that, though, because I liked the idea of winging it with a girlfriend whom I trusted, much more than hiring someone with business savvy who was no fun to be around. Also, having worked with me before, I knew she really got me *and* my designs.

Chantal and I clicked. We had lived kind of parallel lives on some levels. While I had experienced the swinging sixties and the boutique world, Chantal was part of the early seventies glam life, working as a model as well as on the King's Road in London, at a boutique called Alkasura. It was pretty famous for catering to the likes of David Bowie, Bryan Ferry, Marc Bolan, and anyone who was anyone in that seventies scene. And just like me in the sixties, she had to get out before she burnt out. Which is how she found herself in New York selling my line. So we pretty much had a lot of the same sensibilities.

If I could persuade her to jump in with me, she would be the Butch Cassidy to my Sundance Kid, or a Bonnie to my Clyde. I set up a meeting for the two of us at Café Un Deux Trois, a cheap but cute place on West Forty-Fourth Street close to her apartment. I walked in not knowing whether Chantal was open to my kind of adventure. I knew she wasn't completely happy working for Cathy Hardwick, but she needed the financial security. I sat her down, had a sip of the house wine, and summoned all the confidence I could muster. "Look," I said, "I want to make you an offer that I think will be really good for you." I wasn't into negotiating, I just went in with my best offer—the two of us in a complete and equal partnership. I didn't want to think of it in any other terms. Not only did I not *want* a boss, I didn't want to *be* a boss, either.

I launched into my plan, touching on my idea for "A Wardrobe in Stretch," and about this new DuPont fabric I'd found called cotton Lycra. I explained to her that the clothes I wanted to make were the kind of stuff *I* wanted to wear, and there had to be lots of other girls out there who thought like I did and would want to wear it, too.

Then I took a deep breath and tried to gauge her first reactions. She had an absolute poker face, so I decided to just move

ahead as if she were enthusiastic. I brought up my one reserva-
tion about teaming up with her—she was partying a lot and
had a series of boyfriends who, quite frankly, frightened me. I
wasn't being judgmental. God knows I was playing the field
and had my share of bad-news boyfriends, too, but I was trying
to put that behavior behind me. I got very serious and told her
she would have to settle down and leave all that stuff behind
her if she wanted to accept my offer. I needed someone who was
committed to the business first, because I was just *that* serious
about starting a company with her.

I finished my spiel, and still she barely said a word. Chantal's silence seemed never ending, and I found myself practic-
ing my signature on the paper tablecloth. I was already thinking
about our logo and wondering at this moment if it was doomed
to be seen only by the busboy throwing it out when he cleared
our table.

Finally she said, "Can I have two weeks to think about it?"
I lifted my hot-pink marker from the tablecloth and stared at
her. I was *extremely* surprised. I had thought she'd jump at the
offer, but I agreed to give her the two weeks. I didn't know
anyone else I wanted to go into business with, and I couldn't
imagine failing right out of the gate—let alone disappointing
Giorgio and my psychic, Frank. I had to stay positive.

During the time I was waiting for Chantal's decision I kept
myself busy by actually designing the collection. I had been ex-
perimenting with cotton Lycra and planned to create a series of

basic shapes: leggings, skating skirts, long-sleeved tees, and a few pieces that could work on their own or in conjunction with the whole collection. My key idea was that the entire line would be convertible. Meaning each piece worked perfectly with all the other pieces. It was all mix and matchy. And as I had promised, it would be an entire wardrobe in stretch. Cotton Lycra is a fabric that had been used only in athletic wear. I wanted to elevate this unconventional material into something more, something new, and, I hoped, something that people would want.

I had first discovered the fabric at a factory in New Jersey when I was sourcing something much less interesting for a freelance gig. It was basically stretch cotton shot with Lycra, which gave it a four-way or circular stretch, as opposed to two-way stretch, which was all we had to work with up until then. The closest thing I had previously seen would have been the football jersey material I worked with at Paraphernalia. Using cotton Lycra for real fashion would be at the very least a novelty, not to mention supercheap to produce.

When the two-week waiting period *finally* ended, I walked nervously to Un Deux Trois to meet Chantal. I had my designs in a portfolio tucked uncomfortably under one arm. I arrived first and, being the superstitious person I am, sat at the same table where I had made her the offer. I had already decided that I wouldn't order anything until I heard Chantal's answer. If it was no, I would just leave, devastated, and have to rethink the entire situation. Her turning me down was a very real possibility.

She arrived ten minutes late and sat down. Neither of us said anything. There weren't even any awkward hellos, and I could tell she was as nervous as I was. When the waiter came to the table, Chantal—without saying a word to me—ordered a bottle of champagne and flashed me an all-telling smile. I exhaled for the first time in fourteen days.

As soon as that cork was popped and we toasted, I pulled out the portfolio that I had been busting to share with her. She immediately understood the designs. She loved the idea of an entire collection based on cotton Lycra and was totally on board with the concept of activewear as fashion. She even said the words any designer would want to hear: "If I saw this in a store, I would buy it."

Chantal asked for one of my markers, and we both sketched out notes, questions, and drawings that would become the seeds of our business plan. First up, our biggest expense would be a workspace and a showroom. I would also need a pattern maker. I knew how to cut and sew, but pattern making is a very specific skill. I can do it but I'm not great at it, and we needed someone with a real talent to draft for us. We started listing production personnel we'd need to hire right off. And then, of course, we would have to stage a fashion show. Because, as Giorgio had told me, once I made *that* decision, it would *have* to be full speed ahead. No backing down. I'd need to rent a venue months in advance and hire models.

The list of expenses was starting to add up pretty quickly. I figured if we could somehow come up with two hundred thousand dollars we could pull it off. And I'm not just talking about the show, but actually starting the company.

As I finished the champagne, my first naïve idea was that we would go to a bank with our plan and simply apply for a loan. Isn't that the way you start a business? So a few days later Chantal and I dressed in what we thought were very conservative outfits. That was my second naïve business idea. Conservative for us meant anything that didn't have sequins or satin on it. We dressed head to toe in black—me with my punky chopped-up Keith Richards hair, and Chantal with her wild flaming red mane.

I set up a meeting with a banker from the Benjamin Franklin Bank, whom I had worked with when I was with Alley Cat. He always told me how impressed he was with how I handled the finances for the label. I decided to cash in on the relationship. This is how we ended up at Penn Station boarding a train for North Philly

When we arrived at the bank, good old Ben Franklin was there to meet us. Looking every inch the banker in his three-piece suit and wire-rimmed glasses, he escorted us to his desk, which was right out in the open in a massive old bank building with vaulted ceilings and marble floors. The sheer size of the place made me feel even smaller than my actual five-foot-four frame. We sat down and he asked, "Now, what can I do for you?" I repeated what I had discussed briefly with him over the phone. I told him that we wanted to start our own clothing company. I laid out our plan as best I could and told him how much money I thought we would need.

He seemed amused that we knew so little about how these things worked. He patiently explained that if we needed two hundred thousand dollars we would have to come up with half the amount and get someone to co-sign for a bank loan for the other half. Our big meeting was over in five minutes. With the wind knocked out of our sails we hightailed it back to New York and went to the café to regroup.

As soon as we sat down, out came my markers, ready for another assault on the tablecloth. I had thirty thousand dollars saved, but that left seventy thousand to go before we could get our loan. We made lists of anyone and everyone who we thought could or would lend us money. And believe me, it wasn't a very long list. We started with our parents.

My dad had always been very supportive of me and my career. He knew I worked extremely hard and was very serious about this venture. And I had a good track record. Dad was the one who had lent me five hundred dollars to start my T-shirt business back in the *Mademoiselle* days, which I paid back pretty quickly. This time it would have to be a lot more than that.

Chantal was fairly confident that her mother could front her some money as well. Not that her mother was a rich lady—she wasn't. But like my parents, she was always right there to back Chantal's choices. This was the same woman who'd championed her daughter's decision to give up college after six months to backpack around Europe.

So on the same day, Chantal set off for south Jersey and I headed to Terryville to lock down loans from her mom and my dad. Even with parental cooperation and my savings, we would still be short. It looked like I was going to have to say yes to Bayer aspirin. Let me explain.

A few weeks earlier I had been contacted by a representative from Bayer asking me to appear in a magazine ad. Their campaign was going to feature people from different high-stress industries. I think there was going to be a surgeon, a pro golfer, a cop, a fireman . . . and me. (How a fashion designer's stress level compares to that of a surgeon or a fireman is beyond me.) Right from the get-go I told them I wasn't interested. To me it seemed painfully uncool and, in a way, as if I was selling out. I mean, I was always the outsider, the hip downtown designer. Bayer aspirin wasn't exactly the trendiest product around.

But now the money they were offering seemed too good to turn down. I vaguely remembered my mother taking Bayer aspirin when I was a kid and realized I must have taken one or two of them in my life. Who hasn't had a headache? I called the Bayer rep back and said I would do it.

With that job I made ten thousand dollars for the company start-up, *and* my moral compass and street cred remained more or less intact. I can still picture the ad. Across the top of the page it said "Betsey Johnson, NYC Fashion Designer." Beneath the type was a photo of me in one of the striped Lycra outfits from the collection that I planned on producing. I had sewn up a few of the pieces just for the shoot, figuring it would be a good marketing ploy. I was photographed sitting at a drafting table in a reasonable facsimile of a design studio with pattern pieces hanging from the ceiling and bolts of fabric draped over tables. I was rubbing my temples, and the copy read "I'm in the fashion biz and I am only as successful as my last collection. With that kind of pressure, I need a pain reliever I can count on" or something silly like that. They had asked me to feign a pressure headache, and believe me, with all I was going through, I wasn't acting.

Chantal's mother agreed to lend her thirty thousand dollars. My father was going to come in as an equal partner with Chantal and me for thirty thousand. With my thirty thousand dollars in savings and the ten thousand from Bayer, we had the hundred thousand dollars the bank required to loan us the balance . . . with my father co-signing. Whew—we did it!

We found a small space on West Thirty-Fifth Street in the Mary McFadden building that could be split into a workroom and showroom. Chantal, who had the perfect body, would double as my fit model and our one-person sales staff. We bought cheap red paper folding screens from Chinatown to separate the spaces. The walls were all painted white, and the floor was high-gloss red. In fact, one of Chantal's responsibilities was to paint out the floors every Friday night. She would start in one corner and work her way toward the door, the whole time wearing stiletto heels! We kept that place clean and as neat as a pin.

The beginning—me and Chantal in our first workroom/showroom

We were both working like dogs. Chantal was still repping for Cathy Hardwick during the day, at least when we were first getting started, and I spent my days designing the clothes. We paid ourselves the tiniest salaries we could afford to live on, so we subsisted on one can of tuna fish each per day and the cheapest bottle of wine at Un Deux Trois to close out the long work shift. We made the café our workspace away from work and stayed there late into the night, always at the same table, which was covered in white paper. All the tables had white paper and a glass of colored crayons. So it was an easy, breezy work-room. We talked to each other nonstop about our progress to-ward launching the show. I'm sure the restaurant staff thought we were a couple, because we were absolutely inseparable.

My dad, meanwhile, was feeling a little left out. He didn't understand the industry, or our ways of working—which were haphazard at best. He wanted to be involved in everything we were doing, and it just wasn't realistic. He couldn't sit with me and Chantal for hours on end discussing strategy or whatever it is we were trying to work out. Nor was he comfortable with Chantal being an equal partner. He and I had quite a few argu-ments about that. Then he wanted a traditionally laid-out busi-ness plan, and I used to say to him, "Daddy, the only plan I have is for all of us *not* to go broke." It wasn't long before I asked him if he would be interested in being more of a silent partner. We eventually agreed that over time Chantal and I would buy him out. I love my dad, but it just felt right for Chantal and me to be running things solo, because we were so in sync.

The next big decision that we had to make in sync was where to stage our first show. I really liked St. Clement's Church on Forty-Sixth Street between Ninth and Tenth avenues. A section of the building was an art and performance space—I think you could refer to it as off-off-Broadway—that was the perfect size for me. It held only about 150 people, so it wouldn't feel cavernous and empty if no one showed up, which was one of my biggest fears. And it had a proper proscenium stage, which I liked so much better than the typical runway. They rented the space out for charity events. We got if for five hundred dollars.

When I brought Chantal with me to see the church, there was a show featuring the artist Red Grooms, whom I loved, but we quickly realized that the space was booked up months in advance. They did have one date available for rent—August 10, my birthday. *Again* the stars were aligning and I saw it as a sign that we were on the right track. Chantal also saw the potential for a great launch there, and together we enthusiastically said yes right on the spot.

St. Clement's was located in a very sketchy area really close to the entry to the Lincoln Tunnel, a neighborhood notorious for prostitution. Girls would solicit guys in cars right by the tunnel entrance, and the guys would take them through to a no-tell motel on the Jersey side. I always wondered how the girls got back.

After we left the church we walked over to a corner, looking for a cab. Chantal was wearing a long, tight pencil skirt, leather jacket, fishnet stockings, and high heels. I was in a very similar outfit. Soon a cop came up to us and said, "All right, girls, move along."

Chantal looked at me and said, "He thinks we're hookers!" She was shocked. But I was kind of flattered. I thought those girls looked great!

My concept for the show was, not surprisingly, a bit unusual.

Since there was no proper runway, I decided we would stage it like my dance school recitals had been presented, with all the girls appearing at the same time. The theater had a small orchestra pit, where I would lay out the entire line flat on the floor. When the curtain came up, the girls would be standing in a row, wearing either bathing suits or body suits. They would step down off the stage into the pit, dress themselves, and then change outfits right in front of the audience.

With this choreography, if that's what you could call it, I was making the statement that cotton Lycra could work for all types of garments: a wrap dress, a dolman-sleeved jacket, a crop top, a bikini, a tight body-conscious dress, and a fit and flare—everything. The collection was completely unlike anything that was being offered in the mainstream at that time. I was giving people something they didn't know they wanted— basically it was activewear as streetwear as fashion, which was unheard of back then. It's everywhere now.

Even though the girls would be practically naked in front of a crowd, there was no question of modesty, because most of the models I hired were strippers, and a few were even girls from the Lincoln Tunnel entrance. I knew the strippers from the Garment District where they worked during the day as fit models. I met the hookers when we came to check out the church and theater. They were all pretty and had great bodies, which is why I didn't mind the cop's comment earlier. Plus, they really rocked their skimpy outfits out there as they worked by the tunnel.

Prepping for my first fashion show

And the curtain goes up. They've got legs!

I had done fashion shows before at Paraphernalia and twice a year with Alley Cat.

But it's a *whole* different ball game when you're spending your own money. You have to get very creative. Hiring strippers and hookers and actresses and salesgirls from hip stores was an aesthetic choice but also an economic one—we definitely couldn't afford real models hired from an agency.

There was a lot to do, and Chantal and I did so much of it by ourselves. Right up to the last minute I was cutting and sewing. Only a couple of nights before the show, I was still way behind schedule, and out of desperation I had to enlist Chantal to help me cut garments. I had been up for two days straight and was starting to get loopy. Chantal has many, many talents, but cutting out garments is *not* one of them. She made such a mess of some simple circle skirts that it looked as if a shark had been at them. I ended up cutting them into shorter skirts rather than waste precious fabric. When I got upset about having to do the extra work and about the potential waste, she burst into tears. It's very out of character for me to lose my patience, but that's just how frazzled we were.

We had moments where we really doubted that we could pull it off, and if we did, what then? What if nobody liked the clothes? What if nobody bought them? We tried not to get too hung up on the what ifs and just went full speed ahead, fueled by tuna fish and not much else.

When August 10 finally arrived, I was a nervous wreck. I hadn't slept; the clothes were barely finished; I wasn't sure if the stage setup would work. I wasn't sure about *anything*. No one was cooperating. The models were all over the place. The lighting guys were nowhere to be found. The DJ was late. Finally, I went down to the stage and just crumpled to the floor, sobbing beyond control. Suddenly everyone stopped what he or she was doing and snapped into shape. In no time the stage was lit, the models were partially dressed, and people started to stream into the room. At least my worst fear hadn't come true—we would play to a full house.

I'd sent out invitations to absolutely everyone I had ever met. I still had some contacts from Paraphernalia and Alley Cat and was grateful that they'd agreed to share their lists with me. Edie Locke from *Mademoiselle* did the same. Every seat was filled, and there were even people lining the back of the theater. The great turnout may have been partly due to our starting off with a show for the holiday season—there weren't many competing shows. Another brilliant suggestion from Mr. Sant'Angelo.

As soon as I got all the girls positioned and had all the clothing in place, I cued the lighting guy and the DJ, who were both friends of mine. I called in a lot of favors to put on this show and now I could stand back and see if they paid off. I'd like to say that the show went off without a hitch, but a lot of the time the girls looked as if they didn't know which end was up. There was a lot of fumbling, dropping of clothes, and more than a few "wardrobe malfunctions." But the girls were all having so much fun that none of the mistakes read as such, and they only added to the general kooky atmosphere that I was looking for.

The audience really got caught up in the spirit of the show, considering how out there it was and by the finale they were on their feet cheering and applauding. Chantal and I were over the moon, and we both took a bow together.

Directly after the show it was back to the workroom. I hadn't made any arrangements to have the clothes sent back, so we packed the rolling racks ourselves as best we could, and the models wheeled them back. This was the start of another superstitious tradition, one I continued for years.

Once back at the showroom Chantal and I toasted each

Musicians Loved My Clothes!

Linda Ronstadt in one of my dresses with her band the Stone Poneys at the Bottom Line in 1968.
You wouldn't think so but she was a very early fan.
She loved to take my clothes apart and remake them in different fabrics.

Madame M.—Madonna photographed
by Steven Meisel for Italian *Vogue*
wearing my black stretch lace top.

Steven Tyler—my man in black on the Autumn 1995 runway. Steven's wife (at the time) and her twin sister were *huge* customers. In fact, they practically kept my Boston store in business.

Cyndi Lauper on my "Guys Love B.J." runway. Girls *still* wanna have fun.

My cowgirl bride—Isabella Rossellini
closing the Autumn 1995 show.

Kelly Osbourne—the classic 2000s
Betsey girl on the runway.

Molly Ringwald featured in *Seventeen*
magazine in 1986 right after she shot to
superstardom in *Pretty in Pink*, wearing
my fish-print cotton Lycra dress.

Naomi Campbell, Spring 1998.

QUIANA

EVA

Backstage at my show at
Irving Plaza in 2004. My clothes
evolved but never really changed.
That striped outfit on the left
would have flown off the racks
at Paraphernalia!

More Stuff from the Later Years

Styling detail from a later show.

Spring 2007.

Veronica Webb, Autumn 2010.

Autumn 2014.

Fairy Godmothers!

My beloved dance teacher/ mentor, Ann Pimm, after a show in 2007. Ann and I have remained close through all these years, and she attended every one of my shows that she could. I can never thank her enough for all she did for me.

Mary Lou Luther was the first major fashion writer to write about me and believe in me from the very, very start.

With my girls: Lulu, Ella, and Layla in the Eloise Suite at the Plaza Hotel, which I decorated.

My Lower Fifth Avenue apartment. This was my first real grown-up home and the place where I really started to spread my wings as a decorator.

Top: Betseyville, my Mexico home and favorite place to be.

Bottom: Malibu Betsey! Casually sitting around my little pink doll house—still obsessively collecting . . . obviously! My happy place today.

other, and I told her right there, midsip, that I was leaving the next morning for two weeks in Mexico. She choked on her champagne and just looked at me and started laughing and said, "Oh, very funny! You're joking, right?" "No," I told her, "I'm serious. I'm done. It's your turn. Now we gotta sell this shit." She looked like a deer caught in the headlights. I told her she had nothing to worry about. The show had gone great, the crowd seemed to love it, and there were plenty of buyers there. We even got on the cover of *Women's Wear Daily*. I told Chantal I would see her in two weeks. I had no intention of checking up on her. Equal partners, remember? She could go away on her own trip as soon as the selling was done. Which, confidentially, it never is.

When I returned to New York, I was sunburnt, rested, and eager to get started on my next collection. I couldn't wait to get to the showroom to see how the line had performed. When I arrived at nine a.m., Chantal had already opened, and the place looked as if it had seen some action. She was relieved to see me, but the news wasn't great. Buyers *had* come to look at the collection, but there were practically zero sales. Pat Field had bought a handful of styles for her store on Eighth Street, but that was it. We now faced new worst fears coming true. The stuff was a little too far out.

The lack of interest in the line surprised me because the show had been so well received. All the papers were saying stuff like "Betsey is back!" But when that initial wave of praise passed, it seemed as if no one actually wanted to wear the clothes, which in my heart of hearts I truly didn't believe could be true.

I was furious about the lack of sales. I knew the designs were good and I knew in my gut that the time was right. Maybe we just didn't know how or where to look for the right buyers. I don't know how much more I thought she could have done. I wanted Chantal to call all of her old clients from her time at Cathy Hardwick. But they were hardly the same customers for *my* clothes.

That night we went back to Un Deux Trois, and I planned to have it out with Chantal. I wanted to discuss the sales situation and was ready to blame her, but she was having none of it. She would apologize, and that was it. She wouldn't give me the fight I wanted, and I mistook that for a lack of interest. It was the first time we had ever had a major disagreement. To this day I feel awful for lashing out at her. I was just as much to blame, or should I say, neither of us was to blame. We simply were ahead of our time and hadn't found "our girl" yet.

A few days later, as luck would have it, the good people from Fiorucci paid us a visit, right out of the blue. Their buyers had been at the show and only now had a chance to come see the line. Fiorucci was a boutique on Fifty-Ninth Street, right around the corner from Bloomingdale's, but it was miles away in terms of concept. It wasn't a big department store but a huge, crazy boutique, disco-sexy in a very Italian, European way—making it the most happening place at the time. It was owned by the great Elio Fiorucci, who created what he called the "New Happy Sexy Girl."

Fiorucci was the one store that could really get us off the ground, and its blessing could mean everything. It was also validation that I was on to something, that I was doing something right. They placed such a large order that they even suggested giving us our own section in the store and launching it with a party and live models in the windows. Of course, this was right up my alley as we had done the same thing lots of times at Paraphernalia.

Coming down off such a high wasn't easy, but I had to start in on the second collection right away so that it would be ready in time for the next six-month fashion cycle. I realized very early on in my career that the whole fashion business is like a roller coaster that you really love: as soon as one ride is over, you get back on for another.

With the second collection I knew I wanted to remain true to what had worked the first time around, but I also wanted to expand on the idea. So I designed a line that retained most of the basic shapes and fabrication and added a few more. The big change was the color—I wanted to try a very different palette. Where before it was punk-rock black and white or red and white or all black, this collection would be turquoise and black and hot pink and black. And after seeing the B-52's at CBGBs, with Kate Pierson and Cindy Wilson wearing Day-Glo bathing suits

Out and about with Chantal after my Spring '80 fashion show

With my old friend Robert Mapplethorpe in 1985 just a few years before he passed away from AIDS. Such a tragedy. He was brilliant!

onstage, I was like, *Yup, that's what I'm gonna do.* That would be my twist for this collection.

Neither Chantal nor I knew anything about projecting how many of each garment to cut.

I had never had to worry about that aspect of design before. At Paraphernalia we were only cutting in small numbers—as many as could be sold in one week at our one store. At Alley Cat I had nothing to do with production. The garments were mass-produced, and an entire department was responsible for that end of it. Now that we were on our own, determining production numbers was a real wake-up call, and one that we should've anticipated.

Chantal came up with a formula based on no particular kind of reality. She figured that if we had even two customers in every state, then we needed to cut a hundred pieces of each style. See? Like I said, based on nothing. But she figured we had to base our logic on *something*, so we weren't just pulling numbers out of thin air. I understood and agreed with that thinking.

Well, we blew it. The collection was a complete failure. We had a couple of small stores in New York City buy a few pieces, but not enough to make even a small dent in our inventory. For the most part, nobody wanted this pink and turquoise collection. Even with our huge success with the first collection, Fiorucci didn't come knocking this time. I guess people weren't ready for Day-Glo, which, granted, is pretty much impossible to wear. Chantal could not sell it to save her life—our lives!

This time I knew better than to blame Chantal. We discussed it like adults and decided that she and I would fly to Europe and literally go door to door, from boutique to boutique, and try to offload the collection. Based on our success at Fiorrucci, we knew we were big with the Italians, so that's where we went. We eventually sold a lot of our inventory at heavily discounted prices. I wanted both of us to go into the shops and chat up the clothes, but Chantal knew better. She was a Taurus and therefore much more practical than me. She made me wait down the street while she struck the deals. I would have practically given the clothes away.

This second collection taught us both a very valuable lesson, one that I've carried with me for the rest of my career: you are only as good as your last sale. Nobody buys something because they liked what you did a couple of seasons ago; that would be insane. You have to move on, and you have to *keep going* with something different and salable.

I may have been feeling way too many growing pains and running low on cash, but I have always been in my own way a businesswoman. Or, should I say, in one way or another, I have always been *in* business—as far back as I can remember. *Literally* as far back.

Remember when I was four years old I charged for dance classes and recitals in the backyard. When I was fourteen, I ran my own dancing school. I designed and sold T-shirts and dresses at *Mademoiselle.* I opened Betsey Bunky Nini. I wasn't gonna let a little thing like one far-out collection get me down. I was going to keep going.

As I said, we sold a lot of the overstock, but not *all* of it. We still had bags of stuff and no clue what to do with it. Enter that lucky star I keep mentioning. I happened to run into Annie Flanders on the street one day. Annie was an old friend and the style editor of a small downtown magazine called the *SoHo Weekly News* and a big supporter of my work since the very beginning. I filled her in on what was going on with me and my predicament. She thought the only logical decision would be to open a shop. She said that she was constantly running into girls who loved my stuff and wanted to know where they could buy it, and it just made sense to have my own store. Also, she added, I wouldn't be at the mercy of someone else's (i.e., boutique owners') whims. I could call all the shots. Of course, this last bit appealed to me. It was a good idea, but opening a store sounded like such a huge undertaking. We certainly didn't have the bucks to do anything remotely like that. I decided to let the notion sink in for a while.

A few days after we ran into each other, Annie called me very excited and told me she knew of the perfect location. A used clothing shop had just closed on Thompson Street in Soho. She knew Soho like the back of her hand, and it just so happened she was friendly with the owner of the building and knew he was worried about finding another tenant, as the space was really small and awkward. This was 1979, before the western edge of Soho was happening. It was still very sketchy, and you could easily get mugged in broad daylight. But I didn't let that bother me.

By this point I had filled Chantal in on the idea, and she was on board. A few days later we went to check out the space. Annie wasn't kidding. It was more like a phone booth than a proper store. Still, we made a deal with the owner on the spot and signed a month-to-month lease. We were told we could move in right away. I think we may have been the first-ever pop-up shop.

Once the lease was signed I got right to work decorating the place. I used the hundreds of fashion sketches I had saved from Paraphernalia and Alley Cat to paper the walls. We bought some cheap chrome rolling racks, and I hired some of the girls who had modeled for me to work as salesgirls. They graciously agreed to get paid on commission, and some of them even bartered their time for clothing. Thank God, because our small arsenal of cash was dwindling fast.

Given the dangerous neighborhood we were in, I worried about the girls' safety as most of them were strippers and definitely looked the part. I didn't have to worry for long. The store was located right next door to an Italian social club, and the guys who hung out on folding chairs in front kept an eye on them. Not in a creepy way. But in a loving, sweet, and protective way. Nobody walks by an Italian social club and harasses anyone!

Annie's prediction was right on the money. People flocked to the store, and I had to work day and night to keep it stocked. Annie was so enthusiastic that she wrote a story about the shop for her paper, even featuring us on the cover with the headline "I've Seen the Future and Its Name Is Betsey Johnson!" Lucky for us, the *New York Times* was on strike that week, so the *SoHo Weekly News* got much more prominent placement on newsstands all over the city. Business went through our tiny roof.

It was actually a riot to watch traffic in and out of the store from across the street. If we had more than two customers at a time, the salesgirl working that day, decked out head to toe in striped Lycra of course, had to step out onto the sidewalk. Those girls spent a lot of time outside. And before long they were joined by more customers, waiting their turn to go inside and shop.

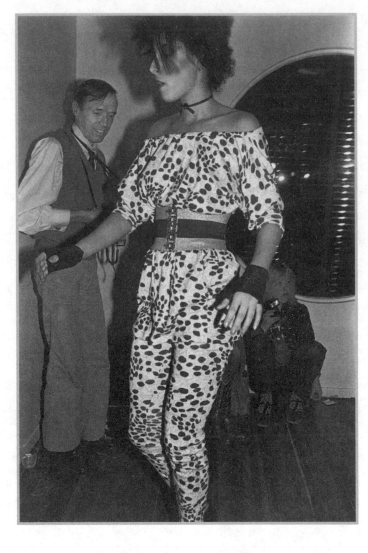

Spring 1979 model with my dear, dear friend Bill Cunningham

First collection with girlfriends and Chantal (far right)!

After about six months it was crystal clear that we had outgrown the little space and kept our eyes open for a new one. Word of mouth had brought girls to our seedy little block in Soho, so we didn't want to stray too far. And we didn't. Without doing any research at all I found what we were looking for right up the street. This time a pet shop had recently gone out of business, and I immediately jumped on the chance and called the real estate agent listed on a poster in the window.

Now we were going to have to sign a real lease and plunk

down first and last month's rent as well as a one-month security deposit. Our tiny shop *had* made money, but we always had to put that cash back into the business to keep the store stocked. We pocketed as little as we could afford, just enough to pay our own rents and to keep eating. It was all about the store.

With this new move, Chantal and I would once again be living on tuna fish. With us it was always one step forward two steps back. But we were fighters who really believed in what we were doing. We were the little engines that could.

Now it was time to put my thinking cap on again and figure out how to decorate this much larger space. I really didn't have many options, and I thought to myself, *Okay, Betsey, what is the cheapest way to decorate?* And then it came to me: color. The cheapest and easiest way to decorate is with paint. And the most effective way would be to do it in the most *hit-you-over-the-head* way possible. I thought about the loft I was living in at the time, the one I had recently painted hot pink. Hey! That would work for the store as well. I painted the walls and ceiling the same shade and bought more black-and-white peel-and-stick tiles for the floor. That's how the formula I would wind up using in my stores for many years came about. It may have been born of desperation, but it looked great!

For my last little bit of decorating I hung up an original portrait that Andy Warhol had done of me years earlier in the back room of Max's Kansas City. (Oddly enough that was one of the handful of times I had actually met Andy. As I said much earlier, I was not a fan of going to the Factory.) It was a crude drawing done on a cocktail napkin but it *was* signed. I'd had it framed way back when and never knew quite what to do with it. The wall behind the cash register seemed like the perfect spot to show it off. It hung there for about three days before someone stole it. Shit!

How to Meet, Marry, and Divorce in Three Months: Husband Number Two

Not long after opening the Thompson Street store, I found I was spending a lot more time in Soho than ever before. Being a creature of habit, I started getting my morning coffee every day at a café down the street from the store called the Cupping Room. Always the same, black with two Sweet'N Lows, paper cup to go.

There was a really cute guy named Jeff who worked behind the counter as a burger flipper. He had long, curly, flopsy-mopsy hair and *huge* brown eyes. I got chatty with him and flirted on a daily basis. Eventually, I started getting my coffee to stay. After about a week or so we were dating.

I may have been focused on my new business and my first store, but I could *always* find time for romance. And why not? The balance between business and pleasure has always been super important to me.

The relationship with Jeff was no big deal. In fact, it was the most lightweight, superficial thing you can imagine. Dating him was like having a vacation boyfriend—adorable to look at but nothing *at all* to talk about. I didn't even care that we weren't having great sex, because he was just *so* great to look at, and that was enough.

That said, and before I knew what was happening, he moved in with me at my loft on Church Street. You know how it goes, they start staying over more and more and going home less and less, until you realize they haven't gone home for weeks, and then they tell you they gave up the lease on their apartment.

Lulu was five years old at the time and true to form she absolutely hated him. She could always spot a phony a mile away even at that age. I, unfortunately, was *not* born with that gene. She saw something in him that I was too lovestruck (or blind) to notice.

One late night not long after Jeff formally moved in, he came home absolutely drunk out of his mind, stumbled into my Japanese folding screen, and sent it crashing to the floor. Shouting and muttering, he started throwing anything breakable. Half asleep, I wondered whether it was my porcelain dolls or my vintage art glass that he was hurling across the loft. Not that it mattered. Lulu had been sleeping next to me and just then woke up terrified.

I didn't waste a minute. I grabbed Lulu, and we raced out the door in our nightgowns, got into a cab, and hightailed it up to Chantal's apartment, where I knew there was a place on her couch for us. She always welcomed me when I needed a safe haven.

The next morning Jeff called, apologizing profusely. He was crying and saying it would never happen again and, like a fool, I believed him. I forgave him. But Lulu never did.

And it's probably no surprise to anyone that this wasn't the only time he got drunk and went berserk in my home. But I was a sucker for his making it all up to me the following day. After one such episode—no better or worse than any other— he asked me to marry him. I have no idea why I said yes, but I did.

I certainly had marriage on the brain, because that's what I was designing at the time—a collection for an entire wedding party: the bride, the bridesmaids, the hot ex-girlfriend, and, of course, the flower girls. In my head, getting married now made perfect sense, and Jeff just happened to be in the picture with me. Maybe at some level I thought getting married would be good for business. What an idea—showcasing my latest collection at my own wedding.

When I married John Cale, it was at City Hall. This time I wanted the big church wedding I'd always dreamt of as a little girl. I chose the beautiful Unitarian Church of All Souls uptown on Lexington Avenue for the ceremony. The interior is all pristine white, just gorgeous, very traditional, and just made for a wedding.

*After the wedding of what would end up being a
(thankfully) very short marriage*

It all should have been perfect. My father walked me down
the aisle. Chantal and Sally were my maids of honor, the girls
from my store were my bridesmaids, and Lulu was my flower
girl. Each of them was wearing a different dress from my
"bridal" collection. Lulu's was an exact copy of mine, which
was made of shiny white spandex with a full sweeping skirt,
layers of crinolines underneath, and the most ridiculously huge

puffed sleeves you could imagine. Right before the ceremony I sewed inflated balloons into those giant sleeves. When the minister pronounced us man and wife, I whipped out a giant hat pin and popped them! Don't think the irony is lost on me at what a prophetic sign that balloon popping was! A real omen of things to come . . . very soon.

After the ceremony it was off to downtown for the reception at a great big loft/event space called Schmidt's on Broome Street in Soho. The room wasn't fancy at all, so we had decorated it the day before with hundreds of white balloons and miles of white tulle draped from floor to ceiling. It certainly looked festive, even if the mood was exactly the opposite.

Lulu was miserable all day. I have a picture of the two of us at the reception in which she's crying and I'm consoling her. Aside from her not wanting me to marry Jeff, someone had given her a beautiful bride doll, and one of the out-of-control guests had ripped it out of her hands and tore the legs off it. My heart just melted as poor Lulu couldn't make sense of why someone would do that. Thank God my family was there. In the middle of all the downtown craziness they were a big comfort for her, a bit of normalcy in the midst of my wacky world.

During the reception Jeff spent no time with his new bride. I felt as if he was even going out of his way to avoid me. A few people, including Chantal, pulled me aside to say that they thought he might be high. I told them that of course he wasn't high—he was just nervous. Which is ridiculous, because no newly married man nods off at his own wedding because of nerves. Once again, I had my blinders on. I didn't want to know what was really going on. Besides, I wouldn't have known how to process something so unthinkable, even though I'd been through it before.

Also, I was too caught up in the actual party, which was more like a media event than a wedding reception. I had hired a DJ from the Mudd Club, and it was loud, probably *too* loud. It seemed as if all of downtown had shown up. Not that they were invited. Word got out and people just crashed.

For a celebration, the general atmosphere was strangely uncomfortable. You had my Connecticut family members trying to mingle with the downtown crazies, and it just didn't work. Even worse, not one of the guests seemed to believe in the marriage. They just assumed it was some sort of joke. To top it off, I hadn't ordered nearly enough food, and everybody was starving. I was at the center of it all, of trying to make it work, and it was exhausting. But somehow I got through the last farewell, and at eight o'clock Jeff and I left for our honeymoon.

We were catching a plane to Puerto Rico, but by the time we reached JFK, Jeff didn't look so well. After takeoff he went completely quiet. Something wasn't right. He was sweating and irritable. I thought he was coming down with the flu and actually felt bad for him. I couldn't wait for the four-hour flight to be over so I could get him to a doctor.

When we finally landed and he tried to walk off the plane,

he crumpled, and it seemed that something was seriously wrong with his back. With the help of a couple of stewardesses I managed to get him into a cab, but he insisted on going to our hotel instead of a hospital. He kept saying that he would be all right if I could just find him some pain pills.

I spent the next couple of days crisscrossing the island with him looking for a doctor who would write him a prescription. I had to do all the driving as Jeff was in no condition to do so, and I hated driving. I'm a country driver at best, and even that kind of driving I'm not thrilled with. At this point he was shivering, sweating, and getting nastier by the minute while I tried to keep upbeat and accommodating. But after the second day I had had enough.

I came to my senses and put two and two together. The warnings from everyone at the wedding, the flu symptoms, and now this back nonsense: He was going through withdrawal, not back spasms.

We did finally manage to get him pain pills through a recommendation from the concierge at our hotel. I put Jeff to bed and went into the other room to call my friend Tony, who lived in my building back home. Lulu had been staying with my parents, and I asked Tony to get her and bring her down to Puerto Rico to stay with me. He was a dear friend and agreed to do it. My revelation of Jeff's drug addiction came as no surprise to him.

I made a plan to send Jeff packing as soon as he could pick himself out of bed. The next day he woke up and asked for orange juice, and I told him we were through. I didn't even bother mentioning the drugs. He was so fucked up on pills that he didn't seem to hear me or maybe he just didn't care. But he did leave without causing a scene.

Lulu arrived the next day with Tony. She was thrilled that Jeff was out of the picture and that it was just going to be the two of us again. Tony stayed for a couple of days to make the trip worthwhile, and I was glad for pleasant company again.

When Lulu and I returned home, Jeff and his things were gone from the loft, thank God, but so were a lot of *my* things. I noticed that quite a bit of the jewelry I had brought back from India over the years was missing. I was furious but mostly at myself. Jeff was a junkie without any real money of his own, just a burger-flipping salary and tips. Where else would he be getting money for drugs?

The first thing I did was change the locks, and the second thing I did in my paranoiac state was to gather up my remaining good jewelry in a giant pile on my bed. I broke every piece apart to remove the stones. I stashed them in a sturdy purse and grabbed a taxi to my Soho store. There, I took the gems and one by one glued them to these crazy embellished frames that decorated the space. I thought that by hiding them in plain sight they would be safe. They were safe, all right, so safe, in fact, that I forgot all about them until years later when someone at my showroom was cleaning the frames and the jewels started to pop off!

I knew I needed to divorce Jeff, but I had no idea where to

find him so he could be served with papers. I asked all of our mutual friends, but no one had seen him. It was as if he had disappeared. That is until I heard from *his* lawyer. Jeff was suing me for damages. We had been married for all of one week, and he somehow thought that he had the right to half my money. He even claimed he had some absurd right to my vintage 1950s living room furniture.

At first I was outraged but calmed down when I realized this was just the desperate act of a drug addict. I knew his lawsuit couldn't go very far, and it didn't. I got a lawyer of my own, and the letters from his lawyer stopped pretty quickly.

After our divorce was finalized, I never heard from Jeff again, at least not directly. I was in touch with his sister, whom I had actually become close to. She called to tell me that not long after I dumped him, he had gotten himself clean. He was married and had a couple of kids and was living in Florida, working for his father. I was glad to know that and I was sincerely happy for him.

A few years later I heard back from his sister. She called to tell me that Jeff had picked up the needle again and had died of an overdose. You hear that story too often, and I was especially sorry to hear it now.

You'd think I would've learned a thing or two from the behavior of all the druggies I was around in the sixties, never mind having been married to a junkie once before.

So met, married, and divorced, all within a three-month

span. It may sound pathetic to some, but the way I see it is, I made a mistake but I corrected it quickly.

I'd be lying if I said I really *loved* Jeff. I barely knew him and what I did know about him—apart from his looks—I didn't even like. But I fell so easily and readily that it seemed I was always "in love" with someone or other. When I was really into a guy, I would always do anything for him. This time I just took it too far.

It's strange because in all *other* areas of my life it's always my way or the highway. But where *men* are concerned? I will admit to having a blind spot.

Expanding

The new store proved to be just as popular as the first one. And I think the customers appreciated that there was now enough space that they could actually try on the clothes, and I know the sales-girls appreciated not having to spend time on the sidewalk. It wasn't long before we had enough money to open a second store—this time way up on the Upper West Side, on Columbus Avenue.

I never gave a thought to having a store outside New York City, where I felt I could keep my eye on things. But after opening Columbus Avenue, we started hearing some buzz about Melrose Avenue in Los Angeles. As luck would have it, the girl who was running the Columbus store was interested in moving out west, and a plan just seemed to fall into place.

At my 60th Street store

We found a real estate agent in LA, and before long she found us a great location that we could afford. I let my West Coast–bound Betsey girl go out ahead and set up the store. The plan was for me to then go out a few days before the opening and paint murals of my fashion sketches as I wasn't comfortable with anyone else's decorating the space. The sketches looked like very stylized pinups wearing my clothes and saying sassy things through speech bubbles. The decor was sort of a grown-up version of what was in my tiny little shop. I didn't finish my work until late in the night the day before the opening, and we had to leave the doors open all day because the place reeked of paint. In spite of the smell people turned out in droves, and the opening was a success. The next day I jumped on the first flight right back to New York.

After the Melrose opening it took us a whole year before we were able to open another store—this time on Newbury Street in Boston, which was the only place to be in that town. The store was located downstairs in an old brownstone. It was supersmall, but we figured it was better to have a small shop in the right location than a bigger one in the middle of nowhere. I will say this, whatever city we opened in, we always managed to be right in the thick of things.

After Boston it was down to Florida, and then back out to the West Coast. In the following few years, before we knew what hit us, we were sitting on a mini empire of ten stores, and a few years later the count was up to twenty. Neither Chantal nor I ever had the notion of conquering the world one store at a time. It just seemed to happen organically. And our system worked for us. As soon as we had enough money in the bank we'd open a store. That was all the business model we needed. I began to feel like the Mildred Pierce of retail. There is a line in the movie where Mildred says, "Everywhere you went I had a restaurant." In my case, everywhere I went I had a store.

We never had a blanket visual policy in the company as far as the windows were concerned. For each new store opening I'd still go in a few days beforehand, decorate and paint myself silly until I was about to drop, host the opening party, and fly right back home, usually on the red-eye. Through the stores I amassed an army of what I always referred to as "Betsey girls": a group of like-minded gals who *got* me and were enthusiastic about the clothes. Apart from that, the girls' only mandate was which clothes to feature in the windows. As far as propping, they always knew what felt right. They were also our own little in-house focus groups, giving us constant customer feedback. We could find out in an instant what was selling and what wasn't, what people were asking for—that type of thing. My pink ladies really helped me keep my fingers on the pulse of what was going on in the real world. In that regard I think we were unique. But what did I know? We still worked so far out of the real world of fashion that I had no idea how other companies operated, which I was fine with and so was Chantal. Neither of us had ever followed trends and had no desire to start now. What we were doing was working and if something ain't broke, why fix it?

As for the New York stores, I loved to drop in when I could and do the window displays myself. Of course, like with everything else there was no budget to get fancy, which was never my style anyway. I'd look for anything decorative that caught my eye—like pills, for example. I could buy them in bulk in the wholesale stores that were all along Broadway in Midtown. A huge bottle of colorful capsules cost just five dollars, and it took only a few of those bottles to make a visual impact. I went to the Columbus Avenue store after closing, armed with only a hot glue gun. I stuck pills all over the window, scattered some on the floor, and even put them in all the mannequins' hands.

My timing, in this case, could not have been more off. I have never been one who keeps up with news stories. If I had been, I would have known about something called "the Chicago Tylenol scare." For those of you who are not old enough to remember the incident, in 1982 someone had laced bottles of Tylenol on the shelves of Chicago drugstores with cyanide. Seven people died, including a twelve-year-old girl. The incident spawned many copycats, leading to even more deaths.

Needless to say, my seemingly harmless and whimsical little window design didn't go down well with *anyone*. We received letters, and customers were outraged. I removed the offending pills and made a mental note to stay on top of current events.

:) #3.

It's not often I find myself without a boyfriend, but in 1990 I was single and had been for *quite* a while. But the dry spell wasn't going to last much longer.

I had a dear old friend named Peter G. who was a very talented painter. Very Andy, very Barnett Newman. He never made the big time, but he was a really good artist. Back in the sixties, John and I lived in the loft next door to him, and I've been friends with him ever since.

One Saturday night Peter was throwing a party for David Byrne of the Talking Heads and he called to invite me. I told him I wasn't really in the mood, but he told me there would be plenty of interesting single guys there. That got my attention.

I quickly got dressed and arranged my hair. I wore a bright red floral printed dress, with a black crinoline and red and black striped tights from my current collection. I had recently had a *huge* mane of bright red hair extensions put in, and since it was a hot summer night, I braided them and added some ribbons.

Before leaving for the party I went into Lulu's room to say good night. She was half asleep and in a groggy voice asked why I was going out so late. I told her, "Nothing ventured, nothing gained." I had a feeling about that night.

I arrived fashionably late when the party was already in full swing. I surveyed the room, as you do, and realized I didn't know anybody there except Peter and David, so I made a beeline straight to the bar to get a drink.

I noticed a guy standing at the bar who looked a lot like a young Michael Caine. Not that I was ever that into Michael Caine, but that's who this guy resembled. He was tall with curly hair, very British looking. He was opening a bottle of red wine that he had brought with him, and I couldn't help but notice how *beautifully* he opened it, and how *beautifully* he poured it into a glass, and how *beautifully* he took that first sip. He saw me watching him and then came over and introduced himself (this part of my story is so hard to talk about that I can't bring myself to even write his name, so from here on out I will refer to him as He or #3) and asked me if I'd like some wine. I said yes, and He poured me a glass. I took a sip and, I swear, I fell in love right there on the spot . . . *with that bottle of wine.*

It was the most exquisite thing I had ever tasted. Young Michael Caine went on to explain that He just happened to be a world-class wine collector and that the bottle we were casually sharing cost more than five hundred dollars. He described himself as someone who worked in the world of "emerging technologies" and then proceeded to try to explain to me what that meant. Even now, I know nothing about computers, so it was all Greek to me.

While I may have had no idea what He was talking about, I really *enjoyed* listening to him talk. He was *so* passionate. In spite of my indifference to his looks, I found myself developing an attraction to him. He had style and charisma. Every inch the classic, dapper Englishman but with a little bit of a twist. There was also something about him—and I couldn't put my finger on it—that seemed a bit off. He had a weird way of staring right through me when I was speaking that made me uncomfortable.

I wasn't sure if He knew who I was and I'm pretty sure He didn't ask me what I did for a living, which, given my Raggedy Ann outfit, was a shock. It wasn't until later that I found out He knew exactly who I was. Peter had briefed him about me and wanted us to meet.

We continued talking—or, rather, *He* continued to talk—and I continued to listen.

Before I knew it, it was late and the party was winding down. I realized I had spent the entire time exclusively with him and drinking more of that incredible wine. When I told him I had to leave, He asked if He could see me again. I said sure and we exchanged phone numbers. I had no desire to jump into bed with him, I just found him intriguing.

He called a few days later and asked me to dinner. We didn't go anywhere special, just my usual Italian place down the block from my apartment where I had dinner most nights.

That's how it started. I didn't feel as if I was being courted or romanced. We simply *fell in* with each other. It was all just kind of comfortable, and after a while, I have to admit, He did start to grow on me.

Did I mention that He was incredibly rich? As it turns out, not only had He been involved in the tech industry, but the company He owned had actually developed the software or whatever it is that allows verbal communications with computers, making a ton of money along the way. I did like the fact that He had his own money. This was a first for me. With all of my previous boyfriends and my last husband, I was always the one footing the bill, so this was a nice change. Now—for the time being, anyway—He was semiretired and seemed to have lots of leisure time on his hands. So much so that He began to want me to skip work and spend more time with him. That was a *huge* no-no in my book.

We began a long-distance relationship and split our time, or should I say, I split my time, flying every other weekend to one of his homes in Palo Alto, Jamaica, or Yorkshire. It was a lot to handle on top of my full workload, but the castles and the Concorde were pretty easy to get used to. The way He lived was on a whole different level. Now don't get me wrong, I enjoy my money but I don't throw it around. I don't live extravagantly. He really lived the jet-set lifestyle and acted every bit the eccentric billionaire. For example, whenever He arrived in New York, He liked to water-ski into the city from the airport—weather permitting, of course.

I enjoyed some of his homes more than others. The Yorkshire house, for example, I loved. We played the roles of lord and lady of the manor to the max and led a very glamorous existence there. I even had a completely different wardrobe for that house. I wore these long lace dresses that had hundreds of buttons up the front. They made me feel like Guinevere, Maid Marian, or Juliet.

At the beginning of the relationship, I guess what you'd call the honeymoon phase, the house was always filled with fresh flowers when I arrived, and He would shower me with gifts. There was a lot of fancy, expensive jewelry—diamond-encrusted bracelets, stuff like that. Which is not normally my style but, again, a girl can get used to these things! He even gave me a gorgeous vintage car. It was an Alvis, which are very rare, so beautiful to look at but impossible to drive as it had no power steering, no power *anything*. Even if I could've handled it, my feet couldn't reach the pedals. He ended up using the car just to drive around his property.

The house itself wasn't precisely a castle, but I would describe it as castlesque. It was made of stone and had all these arched windows with pointy tops. One of my favorite rooms was the *huge* wine cellar. Even the key to the door was gigantic. It was an old skeleton key about as long as my forearm. I used to love to go down there to select a few bottles, and it wasn't unusual for us to go through two thousand dollars' worth of wine in one weekend. I have to admit I learned a lot about good wine and especially good champagne as we became real aficionados in Yorkshire.

In Palo Alto, He had a more modest house—a smallish ranch-style home, really basic. I asked him to let me redecorate, and I did it up like an English country manor, covering most of the walls with gorgeous cabbage rose–printed wallpaper. I spent most of my time when in Palo Alto antiquing to fill the house with just the right furniture. The decorating wasn't only something I loved to do, it was also a nice distraction from him and the ex.

His ex-girlfriend Jane lived right down the street with their two children. As much as I loved the house when I finished decorating it, whenever we were in Palo Alto, it was as if Jane and the kids lived with us, too. She was always letting herself in, and it wasn't unusual for me to walk into the kitchen and find her rifling through the refrigerator.

I actually wouldn't have minded if she had been nice to me, but she wasn't. I really couldn't blame *her*. What woman would be pleasant in that situation? She was rude and condescending. She took her cues from him and pretty quickly learned how to push my buttons, too. She'd say things about my weight or comment every time I ate something. I let it get to me and often gave it back to her, which is not usually my style, but there is that Leo moon in me.

I suspected He thought it was funny seeing the two of us make digs at each other, because He never came to my defense. In fact, He did quite the opposite. He had always been very vocal about my weight, even going so far as to make me weigh in whenever I went to see him. He actually demanded that I keep my weight at a level that he found attractive. Of course, it was all done for "my own good," as He liked to put it.

It couldn't have been very pleasant for the kids to be around all that drama. What kind of man would purposely expose his children to adults acting so badly toward each other? It was there that I got my first small glimpse into what I'd later think of as his sadistic side and soon began looking for any excuse to get out of going to Palo Alto. If I'd had any backbone at all, I would have flat out refused, but it always seemed easier to go with the flow than to be accused by him of being difficult and starting a fight.

At one point I came up with a plan that would give me an excuse to avoid the entire situation when I was in Palo Alto. I'd show up with tons of sketching to do for a booklet I was creating as a handout for my next fashion show and lock myself in my room with my Magic Markers. I ended up doing elaborate sketches of all eighty-seven looks in the show to save my sanity.

And then there was Jamaica. He had a property in Montego Bay but we mostly stayed at a place called Round Hill, which was a very exclusive resort. Now *this* place should have been a paradise for me, because I absolutely love the beach, but often when we went there Jane and her boyfriend would be there, too. Why He invited her at those times is beyond me. I knew He liked to have his kids around, but Jane came with the package, so she was there at the expense of my happiness.

Water-skiing wasn't only something He did to ease his commute from JFK to Manhattan, He also loved to water-ski in Jamaica. And I was down with it, too, as long as I could avoid the poisonous jellyfish. We could have water-skied anywhere in Jamaica, but He preferred this one spot that was notorious for these monsters. I had gotten stung more than once in the past, so the thought of toppling off into a swarm of those translucent tentacles was more than I could handle. But He would insist—even dare me—and I'd stupidly take the challenge. I never gave him the satisfaction of falling into the water, but I was still traumatized.

He was essentially a thrill seeker and proud of it. He got high on adrenaline and laughing at everyone else's terror. At one point He decided to purchase a small four-seater plane for my favorite house in Yorkshire. Before buying it, He wanted to give it a test run and insisted I go on the flight with him. We had to drive way out into the country to a small airstrip for the test. When we arrived I saw this tiny, very cute craft that almost looked like a toy. When we climbed in there was barely enough room for the pilot and the two of us.

Once we were high up in the air, the scenery was breathtakingly beautiful. We flew over his property, which was almost prettier from the sky than it was on the ground. I had just started to relax and enjoy this surreal experience when I heard him tell the pilot to cut the engines. I screamed, "What!! Are you nuts?" He just laughed at me, and that did it. I got it into my head that I had to get out of the plane right then and there, so I started to unbuckle my seat belt, which just made him laugh louder. I knew it was ridiculous, too. So I just sat there screaming.

I flashed on that scene in the movie *Mahogany*—the one where the Tony Perkins character takes Diana Ross on a crazy high-speed car ride down a highway all the while snapping pictures of her and not looking at the road as she loses her shit, screaming in panic. He eventually sells the photos to a magazine, which prints them.

After what seemed like hours, but must have been only a few minutes of screaming, my throat was raw, and the pilot thankfully turned the engines back on. I was panting and worked up when we eventually landed. When we got off the plane, my legs were like rubber, and He continued to laugh as He explained that we were never in danger. In fact, one of the things the pilot had to test was the plane's ability to fly using only one engine. He had told the pilot beforehand not to say anything to me no matter how freaked out I got. To him it was all a big joke.

In Jamaica there was a small beach at the resort, and every time we went down there He insisted we start at one end and walk to the other, stopping and saying hello to everyone who was there. The place was a real celebrity mecca. I remember seeing Paul McCartney, Harrison Ford, and Pierce Brosnan. I was being forced to be social and I hated that. When I go away I like to get away from my public self and not have to be "on" all the time. But I couldn't do that when I was with him. I just couldn't be me and relax. But what really got to me was that I was losing my sense of self. When it was just the two of us, He could care less about my business, but once we were around people He wanted to impress, He just had to show me off.

The property directly next to his belonged to Ralph Lauren, who couldn't stand him. I'd get embarrassed when He would insist it was okay to go out to dinner barefoot. And I'm not talking about some sandy-floored beachy restaurant, but a classy five-star place. Ralph was inevitably there to witness this childish, entitled behavior, and I always got the sense that Ralph was just shaking his head in disapproval. I was mortified because I'd known Ralph for years.

So, of course, sometimes I just wanted to avoid everything about him and stay in my apartment for a weekend. Sometimes I really did have to work. When I explained that I needed to stay home, He would sulk like a child and accuse me of not loving him. I almost always gave in and put his needs first—a big mistake . . . she says in retrospect. He got used to getting his way, and I realize now that I helped to create this monster.

The truth of the matter is that He was very controlling. It wasn't enough that He obsessed about every detail of his own life. He wanted to micromanage me as well. He dictated which weekends I would see him and where. And it didn't matter if I had a fashion show planned in two weeks. If He wanted me in Jamaica or Palo Alto or wherever, I was there. Against all of my instincts and past history, my work eventually took a backseat to his plans and schedules.

At one point He kept me in Yorkshire, insisting that I could video conference from there to my New York showroom. I remember once being out in a meadow with a video guy filming me, trying to lead a meeting in New York, while sheep grazed in the background. It was clear that this video conferencing wasn't working and it certainly was *not* going down well with Chantal.

He never wanted me to leave, even when we weren't getting along. It was just a power play that more often than not ended with his refusing to pay for my airline ticket back, and those Concorde tickets were *not* cheap. I realized that our relationship was actually starting to affect my work and I could not let that happen.

After one more awful weekend away in Yorkshire, I had

reached my breaking point. It was late on a Monday night, and the car from the airport had just dropped me off in front of my apartment on Lower Fifth Avenue. The streets were deserted, and I was exhausted. I heard a voice say "Betsey?" I was a little scared, but when I turned around I saw it was an old friend, Paul, whom I hadn't seen in years. We'd always been kind of sweet on each other, but nothing had ever come of it. We started to catch up out there on the sidewalk and I said, "This is silly. Why don't you come upstairs for a drink?" At that moment I wanted nothing more than to talk to someone normal for a change.

He came up to my apartment. I knew we would be alone as at this point Lulu was now old enough and had moved out and had her own place on Nineteenth Street. I poured us some expensive wine, and before long one thing led to another and we were making out on one of my overstuffed floral print couches, with our hands all over each other. No sooner had we started fooling around than the phone rang. I motioned for Paul to be quiet because I was sure who it would be. I picked up and said as enthusiastically as I could, "Hello!" All He said on the other end was "I guess you made it home. . . . Are you alone? Is somebody there with you?"

I was in shock and thought for a second that maybe He was having my building watched or had bribed the doormen to keep an eye on me or something. He had been showing signs of paranoia lately, but this was insane. Also, He had never accused me of being unfaithful to him before, and I hadn't been, until now. Because now I wanted it to be *really* over.

I managed to convince him that I had just gotten in and that I was tired and just wanted to go to bed. I hung up and was so freaked out that I asked Paul to leave. After he was gone I sat up for a long time trying to figure out how He could have suspected that someone else was with me.

Of course, later, after we had finally broken up, He confessed to me that He had arranged for my entire apartment to be bugged. Shortly after we first started seeing each other, He'd sent over a team of people to install cameras and listening devices. When He told me this, I felt physically ill.

For a couple of weeks after the Paul incident, He kept bringing it up. I finally had to beg him to drop it, and He did, but it still spooked me.

I was freaked out but more than that I felt guilty. As miserable as I was at times with our relationship, I didn't actually want to hurt him. So we stayed together.

I do admit, that at this point in the story, you may be thinking I was out of my mind to have stayed with him for so long. I probably was. Then again, it's the negative stuff that stands out after all these years. That's just human nature. The truth was, I actually enjoyed sparring with him, and I could dish it out as much as I could take it. There's my Leo moon again. We hardly agreed on anything and we'd have heated debates about everything. Also, I enjoyed the lavish lifestyle and was actually willing to put up with him to have access to it. Being with him might have been maddening much of the time but it was *never* dull.

About eight years into our on again/off again relationship we were going through a rare "up" period. We were at the Yorkshire house for the weekend, and one afternoon we went on a long walk around the grounds and ended up at a sort of barnlike building. We sat down on a bench to rest, and I just took in the beauty of the place. It was February, and the weather was very cold. But the bright winter sun was shining and the fresh layer of snow was making me feel nostalgic for the beautiful winters I remembered growing up in Connecticut.

We started to talk randomly about our schedules, and He mentioned that because of some conflict or other, we might not be back in Yorkshire until the first week in August. Without giving it any thought I said, "Hey, that's my birthday. Why don't we get married?" Like I said, things were going well between us at the time, plus at that point we had been together for so long, and one does get set in one's ways even if those ways are unhealthy, so my thinking was *Why not?* We had never really talked about marriage before. He looked shocked and was quiet. Then he grinned a wide grin, like the Cheshire cat, and said, "I've never been married before. What the hell, why not."

I planned that wedding for the next seven months, and we split the costs equally. And believe me, the costs were huge! I remember both of us being very aware of the costs that we were racking up. But we were excited to have a big party, and I wanted an excuse to wear the most extravagant dress.

The jet set life. The wine helped!

Yorkshire was his boyhood home, so He wanted to get married there. I think He saw it as a kind of homecoming for himself—the conquering hero. The wedding would not be at his house but instead outdoors on the grounds of a large property close by. I wanted it to be very English country casual, with tons of beautiful wildflowers. We planned for all of our guests to be there for a full three days, with different events planned throughout. I organized a pub night for when everyone arrived and a gorgeous sit-down dinner the following night.

I had been so caught up in the planning and making sure everyone was enjoying themselves that the reality of what I was about to do didn't hit me until the minute I was about to walk down the aisle. I remember a thought coming over me like a tidal wave: *I am making a huge mistake!* All of a sudden my stomach was in knots, and I was a complete nervous wreck. But it was too late to do anything about it. You know, the show must go on.

There was nobody I could articulate this to. Lulu wouldn't want to hear it. She was against the marriage, just as she had been against the relationship all along. She'd hated him practically from the minute she met him. Lulu saw the control He had over me and especially resented how He treated me. She was always trying to fight a few battles for me against him, and that was an awful position to put her in. But, God bless her, she was always up for it.

Surprisingly she agreed to walk me down the aisle, and I don't know how we made it. I wanted to say to her, *I gotta get out of here!!!!!* If I had, she probably would have turned me around and fled with me. I pictured myself doing a runaway bride thing, making a beeline for the door and never looking back.

Before I knew it, it was just me and him standing at the front of the aisle, and the preacher was already talking. All I heard was him saying, "I do," and then me saying, "I do," and then it was done. He was now Husband #3.

We went into the back office of the church to sign the registry to make the marriage official. Some of #3's buddies were there with us. My family, Lulu, Chantal, and all of the other guests were still out in the main part of the church. Surrounded by his friends, who egged him on, #3 started getting very vocal about wanting to have sex with me immediately, saying we had to consummate the marriage. I was confused, as I thought He was saying "consommé," and I wondered why, all of a sudden, he wanted to have soup.

I pulled away and kept protesting, "My whole family is here. What will they think?" I've never been to a wedding where the bride and groom disappear for two hours right after the ceremony. I was furious, but He didn't care. He was insistent that He needed to possess me right then and there and literally dragged me up to the room where we had gotten dressed for the wedding.

Once we were there He tried to rip the wedding ring off my finger. It was a big wide gold band, the inside of which was engraved with the words "Wife . . . and Don't Forget It," or something equally horrible. No loving word, no heartfelt endearments, just that phrase. It might as well have said "Possession." He pulled on it so hard I thought He was going to break my finger.

When He finally did manage to get it off, He threw it across the room. I pushed him away and tried to reason with him, saying that we'd really better get back to the reception. God knows what else was going on in my head. He ended up ripping my dress, which was a beautiful 1950s vintage gown with layers and layers of white eyelet lace and a long train.

That's how much of a mindfuck our relationship had become by this time. Before we could go back downstairs for the reception, I had to find my wedding ring so no one would notice it was missing. I crawled around on the floor in my torn wedding gown, which as pretty as it had been, just seemed like a joke to me at this point. I finally found the ring under the radiator. I should have left it there. Putting it back on my finger was almost as painful as what I had just experienced. My God, to this day it makes me sick to even think about that scene. Sally and Bobby tried to get me to see how awful #3 behaved toward me, but I just didn't want to hear it.

I don't know how I got through the rest of the day. It's all pretty much a blur. I do remember that right after the wedding ceremony, cars were organized to take everyone to the reception. #3 and I were in a vintage open-topped Bentley, and the rest of our guests followed. The townspeople lined the route from the church, and we waved to the crowds as if we were royals. In retrospect it was embarrassing and sickening, and I know it made a lot of the people very uncomfortable because they told me.

The day after the wedding we said goodbye to all of our guests except #3's family, who were staying on for one more day. Suddenly they were an excuse to delay our honeymoon.

We were booked for a small trip just a few towns over at one of my favorite inns, having planned a short stay at a very beautiful, intimate little cottage. When it was time to leave, #3 stalled, saying that his family was still there. I couldn't believe He didn't hear how absurd He sounded. I took off and went to the cottage myself. I declared that I was sick and had to stay in bed . . . alone!

Not surprisingly, marriage didn't improve our relationship. It didn't strengthen our partnership. In fact, things went from bad to worse. And now we were going to live together almost full time. I hadn't lived with anyone other than Lulu for years and was not looking forward to making the adjustment. I was right, living together was horrible. I felt as though I was always dreading his coming home, or waiting for him to leave.

The actual marriage lasted only six months. When it finally did end, it wasn't over anything particular. I was just tired and knew it was time.

It was a Thursday and I was scheduled to be on a plane for Jamaica, and I just didn't get on it. When my phone started ringing, I didn't answer it. This went on all day. Lulu was with me and she kept me strong.

#3 left message after message, and they got more and more

threatening until the final one said that He was coming to New York and would physically bring me to Jamaica. How's that for romantic!

Lulu said, "Mom, you can't be here when he gets back. Let's go to a hotel." So we checked into the Mercer in Soho and hid out there for two days. We were playing a waiting game, and Lulu convinced me that we could outwait him. I was able to call in to my answering machine at home, and finally there was a message saying, "Okay, you win. I'm going to Haiti to sign the divorce papers."

#3 had set up an easy way out for whichever one of us would want to end the marriage first. It was kind of a parachute. The paperwork had, in fact, already been prepared and was sitting in a lawyer's office in Haiti waiting for a signature. Don't ask me why it was in Haiti. I have no idea. But I would imagine it was just some random perverse idea of his. I think He always thought that I would be the one who would initiate the breakup, and He wanted to make it as much of a hassle for me as possible.

All either of us had to do was get there and sign our names. It was his signature that ended the marriage. I didn't see or speak to #3 until about five years later, in East Hampton, where He knew I had bought a house. He looked me up, so I invited him over. He came with his current girlfriend, who was a well-known young actress at the time. He seemed to have mellowed with age, but I don't recall that we had anything much to say to each other. The girlfriend, however, managed to get me on my own while #3 was wandering around my yard.

She asked me if He had been oversexed when we'd been together. Oh boy! There's a can of worms I didn't want to open. All I said was yes and changed the subject. I didn't want to hear her gory details and I sure as hell wasn't about to share mine. They didn't visit for very long. That was the last time I saw #3.

I had never in my life gone to a shrink. It's just not my thing. I'm more a believer in putting an end to a situation and moving on with your life. But after I split with #3, things were not right at a pretty deep level, and I felt I needed some answers. I needed to know why I let this relationship get out of hand and why I let it go on for so long, when clearly, I wasn't happy. The way it ended was so fuzzy. I guess you would say I was looking for closure. Also, wasting ten years of your life can leave you questioning your motives. Why did I marry guys who were so *wrong* for me? All my life I've had *great* boyfriends but I chose to marry the bad ones.

I asked around, and someone recommended a shrink down in the Village. I started seeing her once a week for a year and a half until the sessions got to be so boring for me that I would find myself trying to think of things to talk to her about in the cab on my way to the appointment. That was when I knew I was done with therapy and that I was ready to move on. I don't think I ever got to the bottom of *why* I was with #3 for so long, but what I *did* come to terms with was that for whatever reason I did what I did, and at the very least, I stopped beating myself up about it. The shrink lady did say one thing that made sense to me. She said #3 is an addict and you are his drug.

Remember the wedding band with the horrible inscription? For some reason I never got rid of it. Most women would have thrown it into the ocean or off a cliff, as some sort of liberating, symbolic gesture. Well, I'm not most women; I didn't do that. I kept it, closed tight in a little box buried somewhere with all of my other jewelry. For almost twenty years it never saw the light of day. Just recently I took it to a jeweler, had it melted down, and sold it for scrap.

10.) PINK RIBBONS: BREAST CANCER.

fter racing across town on a cold, gray, rainy, and typically miserable New York City December day in 2001, I hung up my wet coat and took a seat in the waiting room. I was wearing a red velvet, white fur-trimmed skating outfit, because before hosting our company's annual Christmas party, Mrs. Claus had to see a doctor about a biopsy.

My doctor was a real Marcus Welby type. He was old with stiff, white Brylcreemed hair and he always smelled like lozenges. I had been seeing him for years and loved and trusted him. But today it felt as if he was keeping me waiting for hours. Finally, he came into the examination room holding a clipboard and a bunch of papers, which

I assumed were the results of my test. He held them up and without making any small talk said, "Yep."

They had found something, and they would have to remove it. It would be a simple procedure, and I wouldn't need chemo, just radiation, and he went on and on and on. I didn't know what he was saying. I'd stopped listening after I heard him tell me they had found something. All I could answer was, "Out! Out! Take it out!"

And then Marcus Welby told me he was retiring. He'd be turning me over to an associate who just happened to be the top breast guy at Weill Cornell. He assured me I would be in the best possible hands. This news just added another level of anxiety to the situation. I was going to miss the good doctor. He always made me feel safe, even when I'd phoned him a few weeks earlier, frantic about a missing left breast.

I'd gotten out of bed that morning and was about to take a shower when I was shocked to discover that one of my breast implants had somehow deflated. I was looking down at my chest and thinking, *Whoa! Where's my left tittie?* And then time stopped, and I froze. I was so scared, I didn't know what to do. I called the doctor, and he told me to come to his office right away.

I don't know if I was even aware that breast implants had a shelf life. I'm sure they told me as much when I had the job done, but who listens to the details? Well, I heard it this time.

Deflation can sometimes happen when implants are left in too long. Mine had been in for a little over ten years.

I decided to remove the old implants a week later and figured I'd get them replaced somewhere down the road. The surgery was no big deal. I only missed a couple of days of work, and now my boobs were both the same size again, just a bit smaller than I'd grown used to.

But for weeks after the operation I kept studying the scars, obsessing about whether they were healing properly. One day I felt something, something that maybe shouldn't be there—something hard and about the size of a pea. In that hour, right before the Christmas party, I learned I was right. It didn't belong there.

I hailed a taxi to my showroom for the party with my head spinning a thousand thoughts at once. How was I going to handle this? What if I couldn't work? What if I *died*? What if someone at the party asked me about my test results?

Believe me, hosting a party was the *last* thing I felt like doing, and I didn't know how I was going to get through it. When I got to my showroom, I just stood outside in the hallway. I looked at my reflection in the glass doors—Mrs. Claus with a frozen expression and breast cancer. Through the doors I could see the twinkling Christmas lights, and there was Chantal, talking and laughing with a group of Betsey girls from my stores. Music was pumping, but I couldn't recognize the song.

I felt as if I was watching myself and the party from a distance, as if it was a scene in a movie. Whenever I'm stressed or about to start something important, I like to play out in my head the scene I find myself in from a beginning to a possible ending. I try it out in different genres, because as much as I'd like it to be, not everything can be a comedy. I keep re-editing the movie in my head until I find the ending I want. Then I hit rewind to figure out how to get to that finale in real life. I do the same thing with my fashion shows, visualizing the whole finished presentation and then getting to work to make it happen. So why not do the same thing walking into a party with a fresh cancer diagnosis?

Which kind of movie would it be this time? A Busby Berkeley spectacular? Or a *Sophie's Choice* gut-wrenching drama? I made *my* choice. I wasn't ready for my day to end with everybody crying and commiserating. Tonight I wouldn't tell a soul about my cancer. So Busby Berkeley it was.

I counted to ten, took a deep breath, and when I finally opened the doors, instead of saying Merry Christmas! I shouted, "False Alarm! It was nothing, whoo-hoo!" My friends who knew about my doctor's appointment started clapping and toasting me with champagne while the rest of the crowd must have been wondering what the hell I was talking about.

All through the party I laughed, I danced, I drank champagne. I carried on as if everything was fantastic in my world, and everyone helped by having a great time. Right then and there I had to believe that I really was okay. I just pushed the bad news right out of my head. What's the harm? Besides, this could well be my last Christmas party, so I might as well enjoy it.

As the night wore on I handed out gifts, sat on people's laps for pictures, and kept dancing in my Busby Berkeley kaleidoscope of a party. I tried to enjoy every moment with all the people I loved in my life. But every so often when I flashed back to the doctor's news, I would just stop and be still for a minute and then force myself to get right back into the swing of things with a *Come on Betsey, you can do it!* going through my head.

As the party started to wind down, I realized I was exhausted and looked for Lulu so we could go home. She had brought a friend with her and told me they were going to continue downtown to another party, and I was like, "Uh, Lulu, you can go join your friends in a little while. I *need* to go over something important with you first." She could tell from the tone of my voice that I meant business. Regarding the truth about my condition—as with most other aspects of my personal life—there was everybody else, and then there was Lulu.

For everybody else, my gut was telling me that it would be hard to share my diagnosis until I got to a certain place in my own head with it. I mean, why *would* I tell everybody? They'd just feel sorry for me. Keeping the horrible news to myself seemed like the right thing to do.

You know, at that point in time, breast cancer seemed to me like a private little club. Not many women I knew ever went public about their illness. In an industry that is so obsessed with body image, there was a stigma attached to it. I think illness of any kind always has a stigma attached to it, especially if you're running a company and so many people depend on you. It was the same a few years earlier with AIDS, when it seemed as if every other day I'd hear about another friend who was sick or had died. I guess it's human nature for people to want to distance themselves from unpleasant things. I'd seen it in myself.

So much was rushing through my mind. But as concerned as I was with my own mortality, my first concern was for the company. I was actually channeling a vendor's point of view: *"Why should I sell fabric to Betsey if she's just going to die? How will I get paid?"* That kind of thing. 'Cause believe me, in the industry, people *do* think that way. This breast cancer of mine could easily jeopardize my business. I thought, *Screw it. I can handle this in secret.*

One thing I *did* know was that I had to tell Lulu. *And* she had to know that if she told a soul it could ruin my life. I'll confess, I didn't stop to consider how much pressure that might be for her to handle. I just desperately needed her to know.

Her friend went on ahead, and Lulu and I went into our building. The whole time she was fuming, angry that I was cutting into her fun—she had no idea that it was about to get a whole lot less fun. I turned to her and right there in the hallway outside of the apartment I just blurted out, "Lulu, I have breast cancer." For me, it was one of those special, old-timey, made-for-TV-movie moments where everything goes soft focus. For her, it was a complete emotional turnaround, and she just fell apart. She was crying and saying, "Are they sure? How? When? What do we do next?" All kinds of questions. The ones I hadn't even had time to ask, let alone answer. This was all brand new to me, and I hadn't had even a minute to let it all sink in.

I found myself consoling Lulu and managing her emotions, but that was okay. It was nice to assume the role of mother and have the daughter be the daughter for once. Because in our relationship, it's usually been the other way around: Lulu plays the role of the adult most of the time. That night she didn't go out to meet her friends. We stayed up late and talked. At first it was all love and death, but I cut that short and we kept things more general, upbeat and girlfriend-y.

Two days later we were supposed to go to Mexico for Christmas, and I wanted to put off the lumpectomy so that we could get away. But Lulu put her foot down and said to me, "We are *not* going to Mexico. You are going to Weill Cornell! Period. End of story." She was back in the role of mother.

I thought about it for a minute and then said fine, even though I wasn't at all ready to face my cancer. I could only deal with certain practical details, like running away. After the operation I figured we would head out to my house in East Hampton for my recuperation. But wait, there was a problem with that plan. Boom! I had no floors at the East Hampton house. Literally. I had just had the first floor and the basement demolished, and they weren't going to be finished for weeks. Also, I had lent out my apartment in the city to my sister and her family for the holidays. I couldn't go home.

So directly after the lumpectomy, Lulu and I ended up spending Christmas at the Maidstone Hotel in East Hampton. It was bitterly cold, but our rooms were cozy and had fireplaces. We didn't do much—there's not much to do in East Hampton in the winter. And that was perfectly fine. I mostly slept, and Lulu went out for many long, cold walks. It felt as if we were hiding out.

We stayed for a week and when I felt strong enough to travel, we headed down to sunny Mexico—where everyone thought we had been the whole time. No one was the wiser. So far, my conspiracy with Lulu was working.

Lulu was great during this period. I really relied on her strength when I was feeling unnaturally weak. She didn't talk about the operation or the possible outcome. She knew me better than that. It was business as usual. I am not one to sit around and sulk and feel sorry for myself. She kept me up, up, up and in a positive frame of mind.

When we returned to New York after the holidays, I started right in on my targeted radiation treatments. Thankfully I didn't need full-blown chemo. Now, I am not exactly a morning person, but when the radiologist tells you to be there at eight in the morning, *you are there at eight.* You do not miss your zaps. And I was diligent about those zaps!

During the six months of my treatment I kept to my regular work hours. I was busy as usual planning my next fashion show, which ironically enough featured an army of big-breasted *Playboy* bunnies! I had sketches to do, fittings to see to, a million details to wrangle, and, yes, cartwheels to practice. The doctors had never warned me about the side effects of the radiation—the nausea, the fatigue—and it didn't occur to me to take it easy. I just dropped into bed, exhausted, at the end of every day.

On an endless loop I kept saying to myself, *Just keep working, just keep working.* I was on autopilot. In the workroom no one seemed to notice my weight loss or my uncharacteristic lack of energy or, if they did, they didn't say anything. Not even Chantal, who must have seen a change in my behavior. I guess she figured if I wasn't going to bring it up, she wouldn't pry. We had that kind of relationship.

Well, the six months went by. I was done with my treatments, and the doctor told me that I was responding really well. But I wasn't convinced that I was out of the woods. It was around this time that I got asked by the Council of Fashion Designers of America to decorate a car that was going to be auctioned off at the General Motors annual breast cancer awareness campaign event.

I was a little shocked. Remember, at this point nobody but Lulu knew what I had gone through. It was purely by chance that they had picked me. But to me it felt like too much of a crazy coincidence, as if the universe had a message for me. It was time to share my secret. I went to see the CFDA executive director, Fern Mallis, and asked, "Fern, can you to do me a favor? Six months ago, I was diagnosed with breast cancer. I'm in recovery now and doing great, but I feel like nobody in the industry besides you is doing enough about breast cancer awareness. I mean, Liz Tilberis passed away from ovarian cancer, and no one was talking about *that* anymore."

I told her that I had only found the tumor because my breast implant had deflated. Girls needed to know that implants could make it difficult to find suspicious lumps in time—and no one was explaining that to them. I asked Fern if there was any way that I could have the microphone at the start of the event for just five minutes to tell my story.

There were three or four other people in the room milling around while I was relating all this, and I saw that they were crying, and so was Fern! I suddenly realized I had not shed a single tear for my cancer—not at the biopsy results, not in front of Lulu, not during the radiation! But right then and there, in Fern Mallis's office, I joined right in with a kind of joyful weeping, and everyone started clapping.

All along I had been feeling as if I was this girl who had a tiny, tiny story to tell but when I saw such heartfelt reactions,

I got it. It hit me. I had gone through a life-altering event. My downplaying my cancer in my own head had helped me get through the treatment but had also blinded me to the enormity of my situation.

An hour before the CFDA event, I gathered my entire staff in the showroom and told them the whole story. I wanted them to hear it directly from me and not have to read about it afterward. And just as I knew they would, everyone fell apart. At that moment I felt my decision not to share my news earlier was the right one. I can handle a lot—God knows—but I just wouldn't have been able to face those tears on a daily basis. That would have just made me feel worse.

But then I noticed Chantal turn away, go into her office, and close the door. I had no idea what I could say to make it right with her. My assistant let me know it was time to leave for Bryant Park, and we left without my sorting out anything with Chantal.

I walked the few blocks with my assistant in silence. When we arrived at the event, I saw that the place was packed, and the press was out in full force. I hadn't written a speech and didn't even have a plan as to what I was going to say. I trusted that the words would just come to me.

When Fern called me up to the podium, I immediately went on automatic and started talking. I was having another one of my out-of-body cinematic experiences. This time I was General Patton addressing the troops. I was not really aware of what I was saying and before I knew it, my speech was over. The entire audience was on their feet applauding and that was it. The secrets, the lying—my conspiracy of silence—gone in just two minutes.

I posed proudly next to the hot pink breast cancer awareness car I'd designed. I'd painted two large busty pinups on the hood. Those girls seemed like the perfect illustration and the absolutely best punctuation to my story.

On the short walk back to the showroom I felt as though I was floating. I was breathing again and grinning from ear to ear for having *finally* shared my secret.

But when I got to the door, I remembered I still had to face Chantal. Before I had a chance to prepare myself, she grabbed my hand and pulled me into her office. I was dreading a harsh reprimand and hoping for a quick "How could you?" Instead she surprised me. She looked me directly in the eyes and said, "I am so sorry I didn't know." And then a gentle hug. No anger, no judgment. Just the most perfect comment she could have made.

Telling my family didn't go quite so smoothly, but we survived. They would have welcomed the chance to help and support me, and I had denied them that. I was forgiven because they understood I had my reasons—even if they didn't like them.

The day after my disclosure at the CFDA, I made the front

I made the cover of the Post!

page of the *New York Post*. The headline read "Implants Saved My Life!" That still makes me chuckle. I had no idea they were going to run a story, let alone give me the cover. I only found out when Chantal threw the paper on my desk with a smile. The phone didn't stop ringing all day. My little speech had worked, and so much better than I had thought it would. The *New York Post* article ended up being an incredible way to get my message out to so many girls at one time. The message being that girls needed to be more engaged with their health. It's fine to have implants, but take responsibility for some sort of follow-up! If I had had mine checked when I should have, Marcus Welby might well have found my tumor when it was smaller and less dangerous. But I'm not one for looking back and am just happy to have been given this unique opportunity to speak out.

My whole cancer ordeal was over and done within six months. And, touch wood, it has never come back to rear its ugly head. I know and appreciate that I am one of the lucky ones. And believe me, I am diligent with my check-ups now.

I continued to be very supportive of breast cancer awareness. Hosting events at my stores was a no-brainer—the stores were already pink! To this day, I still make it a priority to donate money to research. We'd all like to see more survivors and maybe even a cure, right?

I understand that some women who survive breast cancer worry that part of their womanhood was lost under the surgeon's scalpel. I don't feel that way at all. I'd rather have my life, thank you very much. As for getting new implants, I never got around to it. I didn't feel the need.

So today I'm as flat as a pancake—same as when I was growing up—and believe me, I'm just fine with that.

11.) SOLD!

y 2005 I found myself the co-owner of a large privately owned company. We had sixty-six retail stores nationwide, each one with its own crew of devoted Betsey girl employees. I finally found the sorority I envisioned belonging to in college. Chantal and I along with our core group of longtime employees were living in a pink kingdom that I had founded and we all built together.

By the time most companies get as large as we were they either sell out or go the franchise route. But we were *not* like most other companies. We couldn't be bothered. In fact, we remained a true "mom and mom" organization even at that size. I *still* did all the designing. I *still* made all

With my fashion fairy godfather, Stan Herman, in 1999

my sketches on my old light blue French farm table in my cramped, cluttered little office right in the heart of the show-room. Which is where I did all the fittings as well.

It was around this time that Chantal and I were approached by a private equity firm, a hedge fund out of Boston. They came to the showroom and gave us a presentation. The bottom line of which was, our company looked very sexy to them, and they were *not* talking about the clothes.

I don't think either Chantal or I fully realized what we had built, because we were too busy building it. When you're on the inside looking out, it's hard to see the big picture. You tend to focus on what's right in front of you at the moment. It took this outside company to put it into perspective for us.

They were the ones who opened our eyes to just how un-usual our situation was. They told us they could help the com-pany expand and be more successful. They wanted to invest in us, but Chantal and I would still own the majority share of the business.

This was an education for me. Chantal knew, but I didn't realize, that these private equity firms even existed. On paper the offer sounded like a dream and just what we needed if we wanted to continue to grow, which they talked us into believ-ing we did.

In reality, a few years earlier Chantal had confessed to me that she wasn't sure how much longer she wanted to con-tinue doing what she was doing. She told me that when we first started the company she thought we would have a good ten-year run, max. In her mind she had never really signed up for thirty years, which was the milestone we were fast approaching. Knowing that, I figured this opportunity sounded pretty sweet to her. I was wondering myself how much longer I could do my job—or if I even *wanted* to do it. Thirty years is a long time.

To make a long story short, we signed over almost half the company to the hedge fund with the understanding that they would take over the day-to-day running of things.

And they weren't kidding. They immediately appeared with their lawyers and their accountants. One of their first orders of business was making us fire a number of key people who had been with the company practically from day one.

This hurt both Chantal and me more than you can possibly imagine. We had watched these girls grow up in the business and become successful women. Almost all of them were the main breadwinners in their families, and a lot of them had never had another job before coming to work for us, so we worried about what they were going to do. I know it sounds cliché, but they were like family to us. How do you fire your sister?

They replaced everyone they made us fire with people who may or may not have ever worked in fashion. It didn't seem to matter to them if these people had the relevant experience. The new hires all brought with them their own ways of working, which went *way* against the grain of how we worked and had worked for years. You can only say "That's not how we do it" so many times until it starts to sound silly. We were told to just let these people do their jobs, which would have been fine if they'd known how.

We had had no idea what working with partners would be like. It felt like a nightmare, and we had no say in the matter; they made sure we understood that. In fact, they were shamelessly up front about it. Now, remember, these were finance people we were dealing with. They knew nothing about the retail or fashion business. That said, they criticized the way we operated and didn't understand our way of working. For instance, we almost always hired from within. Most of the girls started out working at one of the stores. If they showed potential or interest, when an opening came up at the showroom we would put them in the job. And they almost always figured out how to do it. We had some bad apples, of course, but we always weeded them out pretty quickly. As long as the girls understood the clothing *and* me, things usually went pretty smoothly.

But the general tone of the new crew was "We know better than you," when they should have just left us alone to keep doing what we were doing.

Cracks were starting to appear in the walls of our pink palace.

There was so much time wasted on bullshit. For example, they had a board meeting once a month, and all of these new people spent most of their time preparing for it. Any time I asked one of them to do something or tried to involve one of them in the jobs at hand, they would tell me they were busy getting ready for the meeting. I couldn't wrap my head around what they could have possibly been doing.

And worse than that, as a principal in the company, I had to sit through these boring day-long meetings. They were filled with PowerPoint presentations, projections, spreadsheets, and . . . I don't know what else. The talk was constantly peppered with awful corporatespeak. Problems weren't problems anymore; they were "challenges." (And there were plenty of "challenges," believe me.) There was also discussion about going after "low-hanging fruit," whatever the hell that is! Chantal didn't like these meetings any more than I did, but at least she understood what was going on inside the conference room.

To keep from losing my mind, I had a gadget that allowed me to summon an intern to bring me something—*anything*—to keep me engaged. It was a buzzer attached to my wrist with Velcro. Once, while I was nervously playing with my hair, which I have a tendency to do, the device somehow got stuck there, so that every time I reached for my hair, an intern would burst into the room. After about the tenth or fifteenth time that that happened, Chantal stood up and demanded to know what was going on. The poor intern had no idea what to say. That's when I figured out that the buzzer was attached to my hair. For me, this revelation broke the heavy tension in the room.

I started laughing and tried to explain the situation to the suits in charge. They didn't get it and just looked at me as if I had two heads. That's what I had been reduced to by this point. I need to be surrounded by people who *understand where I'm coming from*, and just let me be me. These people *would not*.

At some point they brought in a real estate specialist who did seemingly endless research on potential new store locations. We had never invested that much time in figuring out where to expand. If we heard buzz about some hot new neighborhood in a city, Chantal and I would go there and spend an afternoon sitting in a café, scouting to see how many potential customers walked by. Easy peasy. It never took us more than an afternoon to make up our minds. Again, so much time-wasting and wheel-spinning over bullshit.

One day after work Chantal and I went back to Café Un Deux Trois for old times' sake and had a long talk about our situation. We had to decide, for the sake of our sanity, to stop fighting against the tide and accept that it was no longer our job to do . . . whatever. We had let these people in. It was our fault, and we accepted full responsibility.

To this day, I honestly have very few regrets. Signing our souls over to the devil, which is how I think of the situation, remains at the top of a very short list.

Chantal had never gotten the same kind of satisfaction from running her end of the company as I did from running mine. She had been ready to walk right after we'd signed the contract. I had hoped she would stay but hadn't pressured her at all. I wanted her to do what *she* needed to do. I was over the moon when she agreed to remain on for a while.

As for me, I was conflicted. By then I wasn't sure what I wanted to do. I felt beaten down and I was quickly losing my oomph. A big part of me had wanted to walk away. But a bigger part couldn't imagine *not* designing every day. So I just put my blinders on and concentrated on the work. That had always been my MO and it had always worked. But this was different: for the first time that I could remember, my work was being judged by people I didn't respect, and that made me feel *very* insecure. They specifically questioned why we didn't read trend reports. We didn't do this because my clothing wasn't "trendy"; it was what it was.

I don't like feeling insecure and I don't like questioning myself; I don't think many people do.

Fast forward a couple of years. Correction, a couple of *unsuccessful* years.

It was now 2007, and the recession was hitting. Our stores, which had always had their ups and downs, were definitely struggling. Sales started to level off, and then slow down, and eventually we started losing money. Added to that, other companies started ripping us off and producing similar product at greatly reduced prices. We hadn't really seen that happen before. Across the board, business was in the toilet.

Chantal ultimately managed to hold out for two years, but by then she had had it. She went on vacation and just never came back to work. She called me while she was away, and I relayed the message to the powers that be. They begged me to get her to stay, but I wouldn't. I knew she was through. When she got back from her vacation, we got together, and there were tears, of course, but I was happy for her and even a little envious.

I knew that eventually the crash would have to come, and when it did, it hit me like a ton of bricks. The suits came to me and informed me in no uncertain terms that they planned to file for bankruptcy and close all of my stores. I couldn't even bring myself to think of how many of my pink ladies would be out of a job.

To make matters even worse, they told me that I was contractually forbidden to tell anyone. I just had to smile my way through the next six months. I felt alone and scared. One thing that would console me was a line I remembered from the movie *Dangerous Liaisons*. At some point in the film John Malkovich says, "It's out of my control." And my own situation *was* completely out of my control. This line of thinking may have been a way to square things with myself, but it didn't make being untruthful by not being able to be forthcoming any less painful.

When the switch was finally thrown, we were given only one day's notice to inform everyone in the company before the formal announcement was made.

I dealt with it the only way I knew how. I threw a champagne and cupcake party to break the horrible news to the company. I hoped, maybe naïvely, that the sweets and the bubbly might in a small way soften the blow. Maybe it wasn't the best way to handle the situation, but I just had to do something.

There was surprise but not shock. Everyone knew something was brewing. People cried. People were angry. Some walked out. But most stayed and commiserated.

And that was that.

Sad but true

Enter Steve Madden

In August of 2010, just in time for my birthday, Steve Madden swooped in like Superman and purchased my brand. Steve and I had known each other for years from working in the Garment District. We'd always had a fun, flirty, sparring kind of relationship. I liked what he did, and he told me he had always admired what I did.

If he hadn't stepped in, the Betsey Johnson label would have evaporated into thin air. Steve was going to keep it alive with me as creative director.

Me and the Mad Man himself

I would work with different licensees and their designers on a whole range of products, which included dresses, activewear, shoes, jewelry, fragrance, bedding, cosmetics, lingerie, sleepwear, hosiery, eyewear, and even luggage. It reminded me of when I was designing so many different kinds of products during my freelance years between Alley Cat and launching my own company.

For the first time, however, I would not be exclusively responsible for designing the product, and this would be a real learning curve. But I was on board and so determined to keep the brand alive.

To be honest, the results, in my opinion, haven't always been successful, but when that happens, the blinders go on once again and I deal with it.

Television

Oddly enough, right in the middle of all of the chaos and insanity of losing control of my company, television came knocking.

It was actually Lulu who was contacted by a producer who was interested in the two of us starring in our own reality TV show. It sounded like fun, I mean, what could go wrong? Lulu was going through some personal issues of her own, and we decided that this might actually be a good distraction for both of us.

We couldn't have been more wrong. Practically from episode one of what they called *XOX Betsey Johnson*, the producers of the show kept trying to pit us against each other. We cringingly made it through six episodes and were so glad when it was over.

I have a rule that I have stuck to for most of my life: never say no to an opportunity. So when the people from *Dancing with the Stars* tapped me to be a guest, I immediately said yes. I had never seen the show, so they sent me some tapes. I watched them and thought, *Well, how hard can that be? I can dance. I've been dancing my whole life.*

Then they told me we would be filming in Los Angeles for six weeks. The thought of being in LA for that long did not thrill me. I've never really enjoyed spending time there. Whenever I had to open a store or visit one of my stores in the area, I always made it a bubbly Betsey girl party. Being the quintessential New York girl, everything about Southern California was just too alien to me, not to mention my fear of earthquakes. But it would be great exposure for the brand, which was important to me, so I would just have to grin and bear it.

When I arrived in LA, I hit the ground running, and I quickly found out how grueling it was going to be. I mean, I have always been a very active person and had boundless energy, but nothing could have prepared me for the grueling rehearsal schedule. The daily routine was up at six; at the studio by eight; rehearse, rehearse, rehearse all day, as well as doing interviews and other press; and finally back home to the apartment they had rented for me by around eight each night and *crash*. It was brutal, but after the first few days I actually began to love it.

We rehearsed Tuesday through Friday, had the weekends off, and taped the show on Monday.

I was so nervous that I flew Lulu out every weekend to spend time with me. I needed her love, reassurance, grounding, and handholding.

After a few weeks, and with Lulu's help (she loved it out there), I surprised myself by beginning to get a real feel for California. I mean, it's just a beautiful place. You can't beat the weather, and most people I came into contact with were extremely nice. And, nerves aside, or maybe because of them, my dancing was getting better and better.

As far as my actual performances on the show were concerned, I managed to last three rounds before I was booted off. I really bungled the final routine, which was a swing dance. What happened was, I lost my place and timing; then I had a wardrobe malfunction—a pink feather boa I reached for got caught on the clothing rack—so I decided I would just end with one of my cartwheels and a split. The audience went crazy. They loved it.

The producers, however, did not. You're supposed to soldier through the routine and do your best, not just wing it. I was fine with losing and was more than ready to go back home. Oddly enough, because of the show's popularity, I ended up on the covers of all the weekly magazines and gained a whole new fan base that knew me as "that lady on *Dancing with the Stars.*" If nothing else *DWTS* made me a big name in grocery stores.

Malibu Betsey

Not long after *DWTS* Lulu laid a bombshell on me: she and her two kids were moving to California. That's right, I have two granddaughters. Let me back up a bit.

Lulu got married in 2006 and within a year gave me my first grandkid. I was thrilled when she told me that she was pregnant. The thought of having a little baby to indulge and dress up thrilled me. I couldn't wait to start spoiling this little girl. I say "girl" because just as in my case, it had never once occurred to me that Lulu would have a boy . . . and she didn't. Little Layla came into the world in 2007 and was followed two years later by Ella. Two years apart, just like me and Sally and Bobby.

These girls are my pride and joy. Layla is absolutely her mother's daughter. She's ladylike and composed. Ella is so much like me—creative, rambunctious, and outspoken.

When Lulu told me about the move, I was crushed. The thought of living three thousand miles away from my family was not even an option. As I wrapped my head around what seemed like the unthinkable possibility of leaving New York, I have to say, it didn't bother me as much as it would have only a few years earlier. And the more I considered relocating, the more I liked the idea. After pondering it for a long while, I realized that there was basically nothing tying me to the city anymore. Most of my friends had moved away. Chantal was spending less and less time there. The work I was doing for Steve Madden could be done anywhere. The extreme weather bothered me more and more. A particularly nasty New York winter sealed the deal for me.

Without giving it much more thought, I sold my house in East Hampton and then my apartment on the Upper East Side, tied up any loose ends, got on a plane, and moved out to what to me had previously been *the dreaded West Coast!*

Lulu and the girls settled in Malibu. The plan was for her to find a property to buy that had room for Grandma Betsey— ideally I pictured living in a sweet little cottage on the grounds. While she was looking, she rented a big house, and I lived in the house/garage in the backyard. It was small but cozy.

I thought the situation was fine. Lulu had other ideas. After about a month of this arrangement, she came to me in tears. She thought having me in the backyard was just *too* close quarters. I think in some way her idea to move out west was a way to gain some independence. God knows, we'd never been more than shouting distance from each other. In New York, I lived in an apartment right upstairs from the apartment I gave her as a wedding gift.

SOLD!

After a long, emotional discussion Lulu agreed to help me find a place of my own. I was sad that she felt this way, but I wanted her to be happy, and just as with the move out west, I soon began to like the idea of truly being on my own. Later in the week Lulu and I went house hunting, and I bought the first place I looked at. It was a smallish (but plenty big for me) mobile home. I liked the idea of telling people that I was going to be living in a trailer park.

I moved all my stuff out of storage, painted the exterior of the place hot pink, moved in, set about redoing the layout of the rooms, and most important, *decorating!*, which has always been my favorite thing to do.

And that's where I am today. Lulu is building the house of her dreams right up the hill from me. We are definitely living separately, but she and the kids are just a golf cart ride away, and the situation works out perfectly for all of us.

Aaaand...

The saga continues. . . . As I was coming into the home stretch, finishing this book, I felt as if I was starting a whole new chapter of my life as well—and, in effect, I am.

For a couple of years now, my ticker has been acting up and it was being treated with a series of medications. In addition, the doctors had been monitoring it with a tiny little chip they implanted right under the skin in my chest. I also had three "episodes" that at first the doctors thought were mini strokes. As it turns out, the simple monitoring was not the best solution, and just like when my breast implant deflated and I discovered I had cancer, I again found myself having one of those difficult conversations.

My cardiologist told me there was no way around it: I needed to have open-heart surgery. More specifically, he explained that they were going to install this device inside my chest that to me looked just like a little accordion. He wasn't describing the minimally invasive kind of surgery, where they stick a tiny wire in between your ribs and fix the problem. He was talking about a "crack your ribs open" sort of deal. I did *not* like the sound of that!

I was scared to death, but they told me I didn't have a choice. As much as I didn't like it, I knew that they knew best. So as in many, many other instances you've read about in this book, I once again put my blinders on and went *full speed ahead!*

After getting the news, things proceeded pretty quickly, and before I knew it, I was in the car with Lulu on the way to the hospital. During the quiet drive I sat on the passenger side being uncharacteristically calm. I was making peace with my God as well as saying a silent goodbye to Lulu and the girls. I was sure I was not coming out of that hospital because I was convinced I was going to die. And I had to be okay with that or I'd lose my mind.

Part of my reasoning for thinking the worst was that my mother had died during a very similar procedure and my dear daddy passed away after having a stroke. While I am not a gloom-and-doom type of person, I couldn't help but think, *Why should I be any different?* I guess I knew rationally that what had happened to my parents had occurred a long time ago, and that since then medical technology must surely have come a long way, baby, but still . . .

I sleepwalked my way through the surgery prep, and I don't even remember their putting me out. All I do recall is that when I opened my eyes and was coming around from the anesthesia, the doctor said to me, "Betsey, you made it!" I was going to live.

I spent a week in the hospital recovering, and as the days went by, I was informed that not only had I aced the operation, but that as I continued to recover, I should feel better than I had in years. I was also told that this operation could greatly extend my life expectancy.

Hmmm . . . before all of this heart nonsense I had kind of gotten used to the idea that I might have a decent ten years left. Now I was thinking it would be more like twenty!

And how do I want to approach the *gift* of another twenty years of life?

I asked myself, *Are there things I could be doing better?* Well, yes, of course. We could all be doing things better.

After such a life-altering event, I was feeling, just as the doctors had predicted, better than I had in years—revitalized, even. And I realize now that I need to learn to stop and take the time to *look* because I have never done that. As you are now aware, I've always been a full speed ahead, go, go, go, work, work, work type of person.

And that got me thinking, *What makes me happy now? Have*

I been successful? The answer is yes, of course, in so many areas of my life I have been very successful. But personally successful? The truthful answer is no, not very. Certainly not my track record with men. But at least I'm still trying, I'm focused on being a good mother and grandmother to my own girls. And as I reflect back, I realize that I have also been a mentor to so many generations of Betsey girls. I can't tell you how often I'm approached on the street, in restaurants, at events, and pretty much everywhere I go by fans who always tell me the same thing: I wore a Betsey dress to . . . fill in the big event. And as a response I ask them the same question: Did you have a great time? The answer is always a resounding YES! Knowing you contributed, even in a small way, to a milestone in a girl's life is a very humbling thing and that's a good feeling.

I've never been that girl who can just sit and stare out onto the waves to feel a sense of calm. In fact, nature has always scared me. I can't stand thunder and lightning and hurricanes. Now that I am here in Malibu, add wildfires, mudslides, and earthquakes to the list.

How easy it *should* be for me to sit still and watch the sun rise and set over the ocean. I even toyed with the idea of building a turret high up over the little pink doll house where I live to do it, but the builders told me that I would never clear the tree line and couldn't get the permits. If I *really* want to watch the sun rise and set, all I actually have to do is walk to the end of the block.

AAAAND...

Who knows? Maybe I'll end up on a whole new path. But for right now, it's enough to *want* to be that girl who is able to stop and smell the flowers. Every time I try I just end up rearranging them.

Should I put a period on that last sentence? If I do I don't mean to because I don't think there is one

xox
Betsey.

THANKS.

TO ALL MY FRIENDS...

DAVID KUHN
KATE MACK } AT AEVITAS.
FOR HELPING ME
GET MY BOOK GOIN'.

RICK KOT
NORMA BARKSDALE } AT VIKING.
WHO BELIEVED MY LIFE
COULD BE A BOOK!

MARK VITULANO.
FOR A HAPPY TIME WHILE
TRYING TO MAKE SENSE OF
MY WORDS + LOVING ME.

CHANTAL BACON. MY BUSINESS
PARTNER FROM THE BEGINNING.
WHO TOTALLY BELIEVED IN ME.
...AND WHO BUILT OUR "PINK
LADIES" STORES!

♥ MY FAMILY. ♥
PEI SALLY. BOBBY... + THEIR KIDS.
PETER + MOST OF ALL...
+ NANCY. LULU..
THE "LOVE OF MY LIFE" +
THE BEST MOM TO MY GRANDKIDS.
LAYLA + ELLA.
AND MY PARENTS...
LENA + CHICK.
WHO LOVE US ALL FROM HEAVEN.

DOUGLAS LEICHTER MY SWEET FRIEND ARTIST + PAINTER
LYNN + RUSTY SIMPSON
WHO BRING GOD TO ME.
+ THE "LADIES WHO LUNCH"...
$ ANDREA RESTO. TOULA AHALI,
SIMON DOONAN. FOR MAKING THE CONNECTIONS.
MY FAIRY GODMOTHER MARY
LOU LUTHER. EDIE LOCKE.
MARIE GRIFFEN, ANNE PIMM.
ROBIN OF "MAGNOLIA PEARL."
RITA CARD. PATTY. JOEY + HEATHER.
+ ALL THE "BETSEY GIRLS" AT MADDEN.
+ CLOYD CLAUDIA GARCIA MY ASST.

TRISHA NOLAN...WHEREVER YOU ARE. BARBARA WOLFSON. MY SOUL SISTER LYNN. REVEREND LAURIE. GOD. DREW BARRYMORE.

"THE MEN WHO HELPED"... DR. SWISTEL FROM CORNELL PRES-BYTERIAN HOSPITAL + DR. TRENTO FROM CEDARS-SINAI MEDICAL CENTER, STEVE MADDEN, JOHN CALE, SHELBY GOLDGRAB + PETER L. SVARRE. DR. ALAN BERGER. ANDREW GREGORY FOR 35 YEARS OF MY HAIR.

AND LASTLY TO MY "LOVER."

XOX
BETSEY.

IMAGE CREDITS

Throughout: pages 5, 15, 20, 21, 27, 28, and 43: Collection of Betsey Johnson; pages 68 and 69: photos by George Barkentin, *Mademoiselle* © Condé Nast; page 71: Susan Wood / Getty Images; page 76, top left: Bob Laird / AP / Shutterstock, top right: Orato Woodward, *Vogue* © Condé Nast, bottom: Susan Wood / Getty Images; page 78, top: Ben Martin / Getty Images, bottom: Bettmann Archive / Getty Images; page 79: Franco Rubartelli / Condé Nast via Getty Images; page 83: © Nat Finklestein Estate; page 84: Fred W. McDarrah / Getty Images; page 85: Ronald Grant Archive / Alamy Stock Photo; page 89: photograph by Isi Véléris; page 98: Ginny Winn / Michael Ochs Archives / Getty Images; page 106, top: Jack Robinson / Condé Nast via Getty Images, bottom: photo by Fairchild Archive / Penske Media / Shutterstock; page 107: photo by Fairchild Archive / Penske Media / Shutterstock; page 130: Collection of Betsey Johnson; pages 134 and 135: photos by Fairchild Archive / Penske Media / Shutterstock; page 148: Collection of Betsey Johnson; page 151: Courtesy © Estate of Barbra Walz; page 154: Patricia Nolan; page 156: photo by Fairchild Archive / Penske Media / Shutterstock; page 157: © Marcia Resnick; page 160: photo by Rose Hartman, Collection of Betsey Johnson; page 171: Rose Hartman / Getty Images; pages 175 and 176: Patricia Nolan, Collection of Betsey Johnson; page 182: photo by Fairchild Archive / Penske Media / Shutterstock; page 183: photo by Ben Buchanan; page 188: photo by Fairchild Archive / Penske Media / Shutterstock; page 189: photo by Sarah Longacre, Collection of Betsey Johnson; page 194: Allan Tannenbaum / Getty Images; page 201: Keith Meyers / *The New York Times* / Redux; page 219: Collection of Betsey Johnson; page 239: © *NY Post* / NYP Holdings, Inc.; page 244: photo by Fairchild Archive / Penske Media / Shutterstock; page 252: Richard Levine / Alamy Stock Photo; page 253: Courtesy Steve Madden

Insert One: page 1, top: photo Ulrich Franzen Collection. Courtesy of Frances Loeb Library, Harvard University Graduate School of Design, bottom left:

David McCabe / Condé Nast via Getty Images, bottom right: Image Courtesy Knoll Archive; page 2, top left: David McCabe / *Mademoiselle* © Condé Nast, top right: *The Sunday Times Magazine* / News Licensing, bottom: Courtesy of Abbeville Press; page 3, top: Courtesy McCall's Patterns, bottom: Courtesy Barbara Bordnick; page 4, top: Otto Stupakoff / *Glamour* © Condé Nast, bottom: photo by Brian Sanderson, Courtesy of the FIDM Museum at the Fashion Institute of Design & Merchandising, Los Angeles, CA; page 5: Courtesy Hearst Magazines Media, Inc.; page 6, top: Courtesy Hearst Magazines Media, Inc., bottom: Javier Gonzalez Porto for Betsey Johnson; pages 7 and 8: Collection of Betsey Johnson

Insert Two: page 1, top: Michael Ochs Archives / Getty Images, bottom: Courtesy Madonna and Steven Meisel; page 2, top: L Gould / IMAGES / Getty Images, bottom: Pixelformula / Sipa / Shutterstock; page 3, top left: Rose Hartman / WireImage / Getty Images, top right: Shutterstock, bottom: Courtesy of Marco Glaviano via Space Gallery St. Barth; page 4, top: Steve Wood / Shutterstock, bottom: Sipa / Shutterstock; page 5, top left: Shutterstock, top right: photo by Charles Sykes / Shutterstock, bottom left: photo by Fairchild Archive / Penske Media / Shutterstock, bottom right: Fairchild Archive / Penske Media / Shutterstock; page 6, top: Sonia Moskowitz-Globe Photos Inc., bottom: WENN Rights Ltd / Alamy Stock Photo; page 7, top: photo by Thaddeus Harden, bottom: Ngoc Minh Ngo / Taverne Agency; page 8, top: Abdul Ortiz, bottom: photo by Justin Coit / Trunk Archive